Fox in a Fix

A CORPORATE COMEDY

ANIKET SOMAN

BlueRose ONE.com
Stories Matter
NewDelhi • London

BLUEROSE PUBLISHERS
India | U.K.

For permissions requests or inquiries regarding this publication, please contact:

BLUEROSE PUBLISHERS
www.BlueRoseONE.com
info@bluerosepublishers.com
+91 8882 898 898
+4407342408967

ISBN: 978-93-7542-312-6

Cover design: Rohit
Typesetting: Namrata Saini

First Edition: January 2026

Disclaimer

This is a work of fiction. Names, characters, places, and incidents are either products of the author's imagination or are used fictitiously.

Any resemblance to actual events, locales, or persons—living or dead—is entirely coincidental.

The content is intended solely for entertainment purposes. The author and publisher assume no responsibility for any outcomes resulting from the interpretation or use of this material.

Prologue to "The Corporate Fox"

A bone-tickling satire on present-day corporate life, where survival requires humor, politics is a sport, and sanity is an optional employee benefit.

There are jungles ruled by nature.

There are jungles ruled by instinct.

And then there are jungles ruled by **PowerPoint presentations**, panic-driven meetings, caffeine addiction, and senior leadership decisions based on astrology rather than logic.

Welcome to **Junglee Log**, a wild corporate ecosystem where predators hunt deadlines, prey pursue promotions, and everyone pretends to understand the strategy even though the strategy changes every 48 hours.

It all began when **King Chuha Singh**, the lion ruler of the jungle, woke up one morning with a revolutionary idea—most likely after eating fermented berries and hallucinating. SShhh. Let's get Serious or at least pretend!

Standing atop his rock podium, mane wind-blown and dramatic like a shampoo commercial, he roared:

"THIS JUNGLE MUST GROW! From today onward, we will function like a CORPORATE COMPANY!"

A stunned silence followed.

A parrot fainted.

A monkey dropped his banana in shock.

The giraffe blinked slowly, waiting for subtitles.

Animals knew hunting.

Animals knew survival.

But animals did not know corporate buzzwords like "synergy", "alignment", and "cross-functional optimization."

Yet here they were, being forced into roles, titles, reporting structures, performance appraisals that threatened more lives than actual predators ever had.

Within a month, vines became network cables, tree trunks became cubicles, bananas became official snacks, and trust became extinct.

The king assembled his leadership team, selecting individuals not by competence—but by who praised him loudest.

Here they are, the legendary circus team running Junglee Log:

🦁 King Chuha Singh – The Lion

CEO. Visionary. Inspirational roarer.

Named *Chuha* (meaning mouse) due to mysterious childhood trauma.

Has leadership charisma until he opens his mouth, after which confusion spreads like wildfire.

🐶 Chatu – Chief of Staff

A dog whose loyalty is stronger than logic.

Nods vigorously at every decision, even if the decision is to walk off a cliff.

Keeps shouting, "WELL SAID SIR!" even during pauses.

Balwaan – Head of HR

A rat with a strong belief that emotions are illegal.

Favourite hobby: rejecting leave requests with poetic cruelty.

HR policy motto: *"It depends, but mostly no."*

Sunder – Corporate Communications

A handsome crow with a PR voice that could sell expired honey as miracle medicine.

Special skill: turning disasters into motivational celebrations.

Chambu – Chief Strategy Officer

A giraffe whose long neck gives "long-term vision" because he can literally see farther.

Understands strategy the way pigeons understand quantum physics.

Karmat – Finance & Accounts

An elephant who remembers **every** expense since the day evolution began.

Default financial decision: *"Cut budget."*

Believes emotions should be taxed.

🦉 Nishachar – IT & Security

A paranoid nocturnal owl convinced that hackers live under every rock.

Wipes system access whenever bored.

Has accidentally reset his own memory once.

🦜 Bolbacchan – Head of Sales

A loud parrot who believes volume = performance.

Motivates team using military-level screaming.

Has only two voice settings: **MAX** and **AFTER-MAX**.

🦚 Chakmak – Head of Marketing

A peacock who believes all problems can be solved with glitter, jingles, and fancy posters.

Rebrands more often than the revenue graph can recover.

🦊 Chalu – Senior Business Manager

THE Silver Fox – tall, silky-furred, elegant, shiny like he is moisturized hourly by unicorn tears.

Walks like he's always in slow-motion.

Master of politics and back-door strategy. Dangerous in silence and devastating in conversation.

Wears a blazer too well.

Speaks softly but kills careers loudly.

And into this glamorous zoo was introduced **a completely different fox**:

🦊 Chatur – Sales & Account Manager (Fox in a fix and our corporate hero)

A copper-furred fox, slightly shorter, fluffier tail, warm-eyed and optimistic enough to be classified as emotionally endangered.

Joined with dreams of growth and success.

Naively believed sincerity mattered.

Wears shirts bought on discount and hope stitched into the collar.

Where Chalu was a polished sword, Chatur was a hardworking butter-knife trying to cut through steel with sincerity.

Poor fellow.

The Mission

The goal was simple:

To expand Junglee Log across neighboring jungles and convince other animal habitats to join forces.

The real mission, however, was:

Survive politics.

Survive meetings.

Survive Bolbacchan's motivational screaming.

Survive Nishachar's random access deletions.

Survive Chuha Singh's speeches that changed direction faster than weather.

Nobody knew strategy.

But everyone pretended they did.

That is what corporate professionals call **alignment**.

And so begins this bone-tickling satire…

A journey through:

- Horrifying interviews,
- Traumatic onboarding,
- Client calls that felt like battlefield operations,
- Seniors who weaponize incompetence,
- Performance reviews that resemble emotional assassination,
- And the universal truth:

Every workplace is the same jungle. Only the animals change.

It is the story of how Chatur arrived hopeful,

Was broken creatively,

Repaired himself spiritually,

And discovered the secret of modern corporate success:

Do the work.

Care less.

Laugh more.

Never let chaos rent space in your head rent-free.

So tighten your seatbelts.

Silence your motivational parrots.

Turn off your cameras and pretend your Wi-Fi is bad.

Because here begins the absurd, hilarious, painfully accurate story of **corporate survival**—

Welcome to Fox in a Fix

Contents

Chapter 1
Incorporation of Junglee Log

In the heart of a jungle that had long ago stopped behaving like one, King **Chuha Singh** the Lion—yes, *Chuha,* because destiny has a sense of humour—stood atop his favourite rock and made an announcement that would change the course of Junglee history forever.

He declared, with a roar raspier than regal, that the jungle needed to "evolve". Apparently, chasing prey, defending territory, and living in harmony with the laws of nature had become "too old school" for his taste. What the Jungle truly needed, he proclaimed, was *corporate culture.*

And thus, amid confused herbivores, mildly panicked predators, and one squirrel who fainted, **Junglee Log Inc.** was born.

Enter the Management — A Lineup of Natural Misfits

To run this newly corporatized jungle, King Chuha Singh announced an executive leadership team so bizarre that even hyenas paused mid-laugh.

Chatu - The Dog, Chief of Staff

Every kingdom needs loyalty, and nobody did loyalty like Chatu. He wagged at the king's decisions, barked at his enemies, and occasionally chased his own tail when meetings got too long.

Chatu's job was simple: follow the king everywhere, agree with everything he said, and if confusion arose—translate lion roars into corporate jargon. His famous line, used at least ten times a day, was:

"What His Majesty *actually* means is..."

He was the king's shadow, his echo, his personal 'yes machine', and occasionally, the scapegoat for when things inevitably went wrong.

Balwaan – The Rat, Head of HR

No one questioned why a rat became the head of Human—sorry, Animal—Resources. Balwaan had mastered the fine art of popping up unexpectedly, listening to gossip faster than a WhatsApp forward, and scurrying away before anyone realized he was eavesdropping.

He claimed to understand "employee morale", but mostly he understood how to file complaints in drawers no one could reach.

His HR policy was straightforward:

1. If employees were unhappy, they could "learn to be happy".
2. If they wanted a raise, they should "raise their expectations elsewhere".
3. And if they wished to resign, they needed to submit their application in triplicate.

Balwaan *loved* paperwork. The rest of the jungle, not so much.

Sunder – The Crow, Corporate Communications Head

Crows love making noise. Sunder, naturally, took this one step further.

He saw himself as the jungle's **Chief Narrative Officer**—master of messaging, architect of perception, and full-time peddler of half-truths.

Whether it was a failed hunt or a budgeting mishap, Sunder could always spin it into a "strategic vision realignment". He published daily newsletters with headlines like:

"Junglee Log Achieves Milestone: 0% Attrition During Lunch Hour!"

No one read them. Not even the king.

Chambu – The Giraffe, Chief Strategy Officer

With his long neck, Chambu could see what others couldn't—which made him the perfect strategy head.

Unfortunately, seeing far didn't always translate into thinking far.

Chambu delivered strategies with impressive names like:

- Vision 2040
- Mission Tall & Thriving
- The Long Neck Initiative

Most of these involved "looking at the bigger picture", which everyone suspected was just an excuse to stare into the distance dramatically.

Still, he was harmless and occasionally useful during fire drills, when he announced smoke before others noticed.

Karmat - The Elephant, Finance & Accounts

Elephants never forget, and neither did Karmat.

He remembered every transaction, every invoice, every unpaid bill, and every expense claimed from the dawn of time. Unfortunately, he also remembered every budget violation.

If someone mishandled funds, he would not just bring it up—he would bring it up every day, at every meeting, with references, footnotes, and historical context.

His motto:

"In finance, forgiveness is a myth."

Nishachar - The Owl, IT and Security

Perpetually awake. Perpetually paranoid.

Nishachar believed every leaf was a bug (the listening device kind), every rustle was a cyberattack, and every shadow was a hacker from the neighbouring jungle.

His IT policies were legendary:

- Password must be 32 characters long
- Must include uppercase, lowercase, symbols, feathers, and tears
- Must be updated daily

Naturally, no one ever got locked *in* to the system. Only out.

Bolbacchan - The Parrot, Head of Sales

A parrot in sales—what could go wrong?

Bolbacchan repeated everything he heard, especially promises he shouldn't have repeated. He could convince anyone of anything as long as someone had convinced *him* first.

His sales strategy was simple:

"Just say it loudly and confidently. Eventually, someone will believe you."

The problem? Often, *he* believed himself too.

Chakmak – The Peacock, Head of Marketing

Chakmak believed that marketing was not about substance—it was about *shine.*

He strutted into meetings, feathers spread, announcing campaigns that involved glitter fountains, dramatic slogans, and three-hour brand launch events where he was inevitably the centre of the presentation.

His campaigns had zero ROI but 100% visual appeal.

Chalu – The Silver Fox, Senior Business Manager

Smart, sleek, cunning, manipulative—Chalu was the kind of fox who smiled at you while calculating your replacement.

He had the charm of a diplomat and the ethics of an overcaffeinated raccoon.

Everyone admired him. Everyone feared him. Many suspected that several jungle policies were written by him in invisible ink.

He was the king's "special advisor", which in corporate-speak meant:

"He knows where all the bodies—I mean, reports—are buried."

The Stage Is Set...

With this power-packed management team assembled, Junglee Log was ready—or destined—to plunge headfirst into corporate madness.

They had the hierarchy. They had the titles. They had the dysfunction.

All they needed now… was a victim.

A recruit.

A fresh soul to enter this jungle of KPIs, egos, and questionable leadership.

Someone who thought corporate life was glamorous.

Someone naïve. Yet Someone *fox-like.*

And thus, unknowingly, the jungle prepared itself for the arrival of **Chatur**, the soon-to-be Corporate Fox.

******

Chapter 2
The Strategy and The New Hiring Requisition

If meetings were a competitive sport, Junglee Log Inc. would be undefeated world champions. Not because they were productive, but because they lasted longer than geological eras and almost always ended in mild injury. Either physical or mental.

This particular meeting—the one that would change the fate of the jungle forever—began beneath the newly rebranded **Corporate Canopy Boardroom**, previously known as "that shady spot near the big rock." The management team gathered in a semi-circle, looking important and confused in equal proportions.

King **Chuha Singh**, seated on a pedestal of polished stone (polished by Chatu's tongue, apparently), cleared his royal throat.

"Today," the King proclaimed, "we discuss Strategy." He said the word like it was either holy or mildly poisonous.

Everyone nodded solemnly, although no one actually knew what strategy meant.

The Presentation of Doom

Chambu the Giraffe—Chief Strategy Officer and full-time posture enthusiast—stepped forward dramatically. He stretched his already skyscraper-length neck another three inches, clearly preparing for a TED Talk nobody asked for.

"My King, my colleagues, my disciples of growth—behold!" Chambu declared.

He unfurled a gigantic leaf-scroll chart that immediately rolled down the hill like a runaway carpet, knocking several rabbits' unconscious. The scroll contained a rough drawing of trees holding hands, smiling suns, and arrows going in every direction like a toddler's attempt at modern art.

"Our vision!" Chambu announced proudly. "**Jungle Expansion 2.0**!"

The room went silent.

"What happened to Jungle Expansion 1.0?" asked Karmat the Elephant.

Chambu blinked. "We don't speak of that."

Sunder raised his wing dramatically. "The official internal communication termed it a *strategic restructuring through unexpected operational contraction.*"

"That means we lost territory when the monkeys stole our blueprint and sold it to the neighbouring jungle," muttered Karmat.

Chambu coughed loudly to change the subject. "ANYWAY! This time, we expand properly. We grow our influence. We reach new territories. We convince other jungles to join us!"

"Convince?" King Chuha Singh frowned. "I normally growl and they agree."

"Yes, Majesty," Sunder said delicately, "but modern leadership requires diplomacy. Growling creates negative brand sentiment."

Chakmak the Peacock nodded vigorously, feathers shimmering like a disco ball. "Absolutely! Roaring lacks visual appeal."

Chatu, eager to contribute, barked, "We must modernize!!"

The King sighed. "Fine. How do we *convince* other jungles?"

Chambu struck a dramatic pose. "We hire a **Sales and Account Manager**."

The Great Hiring Debate

"YES!" Bolbacchan the Parrot squawked, flying in circles. "A champion of speech! A master salesperson! Someone to REPEAT EVERYTHING LOUDLY AND CONFIDENTLY!"

No one asked him to stop, so he continued screaming motivational slogans until Nishachar shut his beak with an IT security clamp normally reserved for laptop ports.

Karmat raised his trunk. "And how will we *pay* this person? Our treasury is emptier than a vulture's empathy."

"Money is temporary," Chambu said. "Vision is eternal."

"Explain that to the vendor who still hasn't been paid for the chairs," Karmat grumbled.

Sunder waved a wing dramatically. "We will craft a communications plan that inspires belief without requiring actual funds."

Chakmak nodded. "Yes! We shall sell an illusion!"

"That is literally fraud," Karmat responded.

The Job Description Catastrophe

Balwaan the Rat stepped up, eyes bulging with simultaneous fear and enthusiasm. He produced a stack of job description forms thick enough to stop a rhino.

"Role: Sales & Account Manager," he squeaked.

Then he read aloud the requirements:

Responsibilities:

- Travel to dangerous rival jungles without being eaten.
- Convince hostile animals to join Junglee Log.
- Handle objections, negotiations, and emotional breakdowns.
- Attend meetings that may last until nightfall or geological shifts.

Required Skills:

- Must speak at least 12 animal dialects including Roar, Hiss, Chirp, and Passive-Aggressive Silence.
- Must remain calm while chased by predators.
- Must display enthusiasm even while bleeding.
- Must understand Excel (no one knew what that was, but Nishachar insisted).

Chakmak clapped his wings. "Add *excellent fur aesthetics* as mandatory."

Bolbacchan shrieked, "Add *high-volume voice projection!*"

Nishachar hooted. "Add *complex password management.*"

Balwaan scribbled frantically, nearly fainting from stress. "This job is impossible."

The King smiled. "Perfect."

The Species Argument

Now came the truly intellectual portion of the meeting.

"What species should we hire?" Chambu asked.

"A tiger!" Chakmak proposed triumphantly.

"A bear!" Bolbacchan yelled.

"A peacock!" Chakmak countered.

"A goldfish," Karmat muttered, "so they forget their suffering every three seconds."

Silence.

Then, from the shadows, Chalu the Silver Fox spoke.

"Perhaps…" he said smoothly, "we hire someone cunning. Quick-thinking. Adaptable. Someone who looks harmless but can outsmart enemies. Someone agile… persuasive… and sleek."

He smiled a smile that could slice through steel.

"Someone like… a **fox**."

Everyone gasped as if he'd suggested replacing water with espresso.

King Chuha Singh narrowed his eyes. "A fox is too clever. I don't want someone competing with me."

Chalu bowed. "Majesty, the right fox knows his place."

Even the wind rolled its eyes at that lie.

The Grand Royal Declaration

The King stood and roared—not aggressively, just for dramatic effect.

"Then it is decided! We shall hire a Sales person. Preferably a fox. A Sales Champion who will lead Junglee Log to greatness!"

Chatu barked in delight.

Balwaan collapsed from overwhelmed nerves.

Chakmak fluffed his feathers like confetti.

The hyenas outside laughed so hard they choked.

The Jungle Reacts

Word travelled faster than office gossip.

The monkeys giggled, "Poor fox. He's doomed."

The deer whispered, "Do you think he'll have to wear a tie?"

The crocodiles lined up for an interview—of the carnivorous kind.

The wolves sharpened their résumés just in case.

Chalu's Quiet Smirk

As the meeting closed, Chalu watched everyone leave with a private smirk.

A new fox entering this jungle wasn't a resource.

He was an *opportunity*.

A pawn waiting to be maneuvered.

Part one of the plan was complete.

Now they needed just one thing:

A fox foolish enough to apply.

And somewhere far away, polishing his dreams with naïve optimism, was **Chatur**.

Soon to be: The Corporate Fox.

******

Chapter 3
Ek Chatur Samvad - Interview and Offer Stage

Far beyond Junglee Log, in a quiet corner of the forest where the grass still grew naturally and no one used words like 'synergy' or 'bandwidth', lived a young copper fur fox named **Chatur**. Unlike most foxes who spent their days hunting rabbits and charming chickens, Chatur spent his time reading self-help scrolls with painfully optimistic titles such as *"Think and Grow Rich"* and *"How to Influence Tigers and Avoid Getting Eaten."*

Chatur dreamed of greatness. He wanted to do something meaningful, something world-changing, something more than stealing farmer's eggs at midnight.

One morning, as he sat sipping dew-water from a leaf cup and practicing his 'confident leadership smile' in a reflection puddle, a pigeon crash-landed directly onto his face.

"Urgent job opportunity!" the pigeon squawked, wings flailing. "High growth role! Strategic impact! Unlimited potential!"

Chatur peeled feathers off his muzzle. "Sounds promising. What's the catch?"

The pigeon leaned forward dramatically. "Only minor risk of death."

Chatur raised an eyebrow. "Define minor."

The pigeon pretended not to hear. "Applications closing soon! Apply now or regret forever!"

And then, without warning, the pigeon exploded into flight, leaving behind a crumpled leaflet stamped **JUNGLEE LOG INC - WE ARE HIRING.**

Chatur smoothed out the page, read the job description, and felt his heart soar.

"A role involving travel, leadership visibility, communication excellence and competitive compensation!" he read aloud. "That sounds *perfect*!"

He completely missed the fine print at the bottom:

Company not liable for injury, dismemberment, psychological trauma or being consumed alive.

Chatur packed his resume, polished his fur, practiced power stances, and set off toward the greatest mistake of his life.

The Great Journey to the Jungle HQ

The path to Junglee Log's corporate headquarters was not meant for the faint-hearted. There were hills, rivers, swampy lands, and an angry buffalo union demanding pension benefits.

By the time Chatur arrived at the gates of Junglee Log, he was muddy, sweating, panting, and questioning every decision he had ever made.

The entrance was guarded by two rhinoceroses dressed in intimidating uniforms labelled **SECURITY DEPARTMENT** (or what was left of the letters after they'd been chewed by termites).

"State your purpose," one rhinoceros growled.

"Interview for Sales & Account Manager," Chatur said, trying to sound confident but inhaling a fly mid-sentence.

Both guards exchanged pitying looks.

"Good luck," the second one whispered, crossing himself.

Chatur entered anyway.

Reception: The Chaos Begins

The reception area looked like someone had attempted to design a modern corporate space using inspiration from a tornado. Leaf-papers covered the floor, vines tangled around ceiling beams, and a large sign at the front desk flashed:

WELCOME TO JUNGLEE LOG - WE VALUE TALENT!

Below it, handwritten in charcoal:

(Unless it costs money.)

The receptionist, a squirrel who clearly had not slept in six weeks, looked up with twitchy eyes.

"Name?" she squeaked.

"Chatur. Interview candidate."

She shoved a massive binder toward him.

"Sign confidentiality form, non-disclosure agreement, non-complaint agreement, injury waiver form, death waiver form, accident waiver form, and emotional instability disclaimer."

Chatur blinked. "All of them?"

She slammed a paw on the binder. "NOW."

Chatur signed everything without reading. A rookie mistake that would haunt him forever.

"Take a seat," the squirrel instructed. "Someone will call you. Probably."

Chatur sat on a chair made of sticks and regret, surrounded by other candidates.

A deer trembled uncontrollably. A bear was stress-eating honey packets. A rooster appeared to be praying.

"What's the interview like?" Chatur whispered.

The deer whimpered. "First round is written test. Second round is group discussion. Third round is physical survival. Fourth round is personal interview. Fifth round is negotiation. Sixth is therapy."

Chatur swallowed. "Physical survival?"

Before the deer could answer, a speaker crackled:

"ROUND ONE CANDIDATES: FOLLOW ME!!"

A baboon in a tie appeared and marched them out.

Round One – The Written Test from Hell

The candidates were led into a cave-like hall filled with stone desks. At the front, Balwaan the Rat stood on a podium barely taller than a mushroom.

"WELCOME TO THE ASSESSMENT," he squeaked. "You have 10 minutes to answer 200 questions. BEGIN."

The test booklet was thicker than a brick and made entirely of recycled palm leaves.

First question:

Q1. How would you convince a tiger to surrender territory peacefully? (Choose one) A) Offer incentives B) Threaten violence C) Run away D) Pray

Second question:

Q2. Define ROI in under 3 words.

Q3. Choose the correct password format:

A) hunter123

B) passw0rd

C) W0ugh#5tr!Bz@ck&7pl

D) I give up

Chatur stared in horror.

The deer began crying.

The bear broke a desk.

The rooster fainted.

Chatur picked answers at random and hoped fate was in a charitable mood.

Round Two – Group Discussion

Next, the candidates were seated in a circle of bamboo chairs.

Moderator: Bolbacchan the Parrot.

Topic:

"Should monkeys be allowed bananas in the workplace?"

Before anyone could start, Bolbacchan screamed, "DISCUSS!!!" and flew into the air like a malfunctioning helicopter.

The group erupted.

The bear roared, "BANANAS ARE A HAZARD!"

The deer shrieked, "THEY'RE TRAUMA TRIGGERS!"

The rooster yelled, "FREE BANANAS FOR ALL!"

Chatur quietly said, "Perhaps we could regulate banana use."

Bolbacchan swooped down. "YES! DIPLOMACY! POINTS FOR FOX!"

The bear tried to throw a chair at him, missed, and hit the moderator instead.

"ROUND OVER!" Bolbacchan squawked from the ground.

Round Three – Physical Survival Test

Candidates were led outside into a field.

"Instruction," Balwaan announced. "Survive."

The gates opened.

A pack of wolves entered.

The deer screamed.

The rooster recited final prayers.

Chatur ran like his tail was on fire.

A wolf chased him, snapping jaws inches from fur.

Chatur darted left, leaped over a log, slid under a bush, and escaped by pure luck.

The wolves got bored and left.

Survivors: 3.

Balwaan clapped. "Congratulations! You passed!"

The deer did not stop crying.

Personal Interview – The Leadership Panel of Doom

Chatur was taken into a dimly lit cave where the **entire management team** sat waiting like judges on a reality show.

King Chuha Singh stared intently. Chambu posed with neck dramatically angled. Chakmak fanned his feathers like stage lighting. Chatu wagged his tail aggressively.

"Introduce yourself," the King commanded.

Chatur cleared his throat. "I am Chatur, a fox with strong communication skills, adaptable mindset, and passion for building relationships."

Bolbacchan gasped. "HE SPEAKS LIKE A BROCHURE!"

Chakmak clapped. "Fabulous branding!"

Karmat grunted. "Define profitability."

Chatur froze. "Umm… earning more than spending?"

The room gasped like he had unlocked ancient magic.

Sunder whispered, "A financial philosopher."

Chambu leaned forward. "How would you handle aggressive negotiation?"

Chatur smiled confidently. "By keeping calm and identifying common ground."

"WRONG," Chatu barked. "You must panic and escalate immediately!"

"Next question," the King snapped. "Why should we hire you?"

Chatur inhaled deeply. "Because I believe I can bring great value to Junglee Log and help build strong alliances with other jungles."

The panel exchanged impressed looks.

Except Chalu.

Chalu watched him with amusement.

Then he asked the final question:

"Tell me, Chatur… what will you do if the jungle turns against you?"

Chatur inhaled slowly. Every eye fixed on him. Even the ventilation paused.

"I'll adapt," he said steadily. "A jungle changes. Leadership changes. Conditions change. But survival means learning fast, staying calm, and turning challenges into opportunities. If the jungle turns against me… I'll listen, I'll understand, I'll evolve—and I'll fight my way back with results, not excuses."

Silence.

Even the king looked impressed—an expression so rare that squirrels outside fell out of trees without explanation.

Bolbacchan finally broke the quiet. "HE SPEAKS LIKE A MOTIVATIONAL POSTER!"

Chakmak sparkled. "I SEE A BRAND CAMPAIGN ALREADY!"

Karmat grunted, but less skeptically. "At least he understands numbers and suffering."

Chatu barked wildly. "HE'LL FIT IN PERFECTLY! WE ALL SUFFER HERE!"

Only Chalu watched him with calm amusement, eyes shining with plans layered beneath plans.

"Very well," King Chuha Singh said. "You may step outside while we deliberate."

Chatur bowed politely and left the cave, heart pounding like tribal drums in a rainstorm.

The Final Hiring Discussion

As soon as Chatur was out of earshot, the management circle erupted.

Bolbacchan flapped his wings dramatically. "He survived wolves! Wolves! With no armor, no backup, no sales pitch!"

Chakmak preened his feathers. "And he looked fantastic doing it. Very camera ready."

Karmat tapped a ledger thoughtfully. "He defined profitability correctly. That alone eliminates 99% of applicants we've ever had."

Sunder added, "And his answer on negotiation was diplomatic—strategically non-threatening. Excellent press potential."

Chambu raised a hoof. "He understands adaptation. Vision. Flexibility. Qualities of a leader—possibly a future strategist."

Chatu nearly wagged his tail off. "AND HE SAID HE'LL FIGHT! WE NEED FIGHTERS WHO CAN TAKE BLAME WHEN THINGS GO WRONG!"

Nishachar blinked slowly. "He also selected the correct password format. Very rare."

Everyone turned toward King Chuha Singh.

"Well?" Sunder asked. "Your Majesty?"

The king stared at the exit tunnel thoughtfully. "He's clever. Determined. And speaks well. But is a clever fox dangerous?"

The room stiffened.

Then Chalu spoke softly, smooth as silk dipped in venom.

"My King… there is nothing more valuable than a smart pawn placed correctly. Give him responsibility. Give him visibility. Let him shine. If he succeeds—we win. If he fails—he takes the fall."

The king smiled slowly, fang by fang.

"A useful shield…" he murmured.

"A useful tool," Chalu corrected gently.

Chakmak struck a pose. "So it is decided—we shall hire beauty, brains, bravery, and brandability!"

Karmat stamped the floor. " candidate Approved.

******

Chapter 4
Onboarding & Joining - The Lost Journey

The sun rose over Junglee Log with dramatic enthusiasm, painting the sky gold as if trying to distract everyone from the upcoming disaster known as **Chatur's First Day**. Somewhere in the jungle, birds chirped cheerfully, unaware that a monumental mistake was unfolding.

Chatur woke before dawn, tail perfectly brushed, fur shimmering with hope and questionable optimism. He practiced his introduction speech for the fifteenth time:

"Hello, I'm Chatur – strategic thinker, relationship builder, and team collaborator—"

He paused when a passing frog snorted loudly and hopped away.

Maybe tone down the enthusiasm, he thought.

He tied his corporate-approved lanyard (which looked suspiciously like a vine) around his neck and set off toward Junglee Log HQ – ready, excited, and blissfully unaware of the torment awaiting him.

The Arrival & Disaster #1: Security Protocol

Chatur arrived at the jungle gate smiling, only to be greeted by the same rhinoceros security guards who had pitied him during his interview.

"ID card," one grunted.

"Oh!" Chatur said proudly. "I received this onboarding badge in my welcome scroll."

The badge was made of dried bark tied with string. The photo looked like a sketch drawn by a drunk squirrel.

The rhinoceros stared. "This is not valid. It has no hologram."

"It's bark," Chatur said. "Bark doesn't come with holograms."

"That's not our problem," the second guard said, crossing his arms. "Procedure is procedure."

Chatur waited hopefully.

Nothing happened.

He slowly realized they expected him to… argue?

"Is there another way in?" Chatur asked politely.

The guards exchanged looks, then pointed to a tunnel labelled **VISITOR ENTRY / HIGH-RISK ACCESS / PROCEED AT OWN RISK**.

Chatur gulped and entered.

Within seconds, a leopard jumped out and snarled.

Chatur screamed.

The leopard yawned. "Relax. Training exercise."

"Training for who??" Chatur gasped.

The leopard shrugged. "Not my department."

Chatur stumbled out the other end trembling, tail puffed like cotton.

"Congratulations," the rhinoceroses said. "You passed your first security test."

Chatur wondered if he could still run away. But hope is a dangerous drug.

He continued.

Reception & Disaster #2: The Paperwork Avalanche

Inside the building, the same sleep-deprived squirrel receptionist sat glaring at the world.

"You're late," she squeaked.

"It's 8:01," Chatur said.

"We start at 8:00. Unacceptable."

Chatur opened his mouth to explain the leopard incident but she shoved a mountain of forms at him.

"Fill these: employee declaration, asset responsibility pledge, pawprint registration, mandatory insurance waiver, optional insurance waiver, and additional waiver waiving your right to dispute waivers."

Chatur blinked. "Optional insurance waiver?"

She glared. "Optional means mandatory."

"Right," Chatur whispered.

He signed until his paw cramped.

Orientation: The Great Intro Gone Wrong

Chatu the Dog burst into reception like a tornado wrapped in caffeine.

“WELCOME, BROTHER!” he barked, tackling Chatur into a hug that knocked all the papers out of his paws.

“You’re here! You’re part of the family! You’re LIFELONG! NO ESCAPE NOW!”

Chatur chuckled nervously. “Excited to start!”

Chatu dragged him down the hallway enthusiastically.

“Time for the GREAT INTRO!”

They entered a room filled with chairs, a projector made of fireflies in a jar, and a banner reading:

WELCOME NEW HIRE

There was a spelled-wrong sticky note under it reading: “Chaturr”

Animals gathered around as Chatu leaped onto the stage.

“EVERYONE, meet CHATOR!”

“It’s Chatur,” he corrected shyly.

“Same thing!” Chatu barked.

Chatu then forced Chatur to give a spontaneous speech.

“Introduce yourself!”

Chatur cleared his throat.

“I am excited to join Junglee Log and contribute to our growth and client partnerships—”

He slipped on spilled honey and flew backward into a barrel of water with a splash so dramatic the monkeys applauded.

Bolbacchan shouted, “HE MAKES AN ENTRANCE!”

Chakmak cried, "SO MANY EMOTIONS! SO MUCH INTENSITY! I'M OBSESSED!"

Karmat sighed, "This is already expensive."

Chatur crawled out of the barrel dripping but still smiling.

"It's ok," he muttered. "Just a rough start."

The crowd laughed proudly as if they'd witnessed a historic achievement.

The Laptop Incident: IT & Disaster #3

Next, Nishachar the Owl escorted him to the IT department: a dark cave filled with glowing fungi and humming equipment.

"I have prepared your workstation," Nishachar hooted ominously.

On the table sat a stone slab, a dead plant, and a device that looked like a beaver chewed it.

"That's… my laptop?" Chatur asked.

"Yes. State-of-the-art stone-powered computing tablet."

He pressed a button.

The device screamed.

"What was that?" Chatur yelped.

"Cooling technology," Nishachar said proudly.

He handed Chatur a password written on a tiny leaf:

P@55w0rD!74-forest-security-level-omega-hush-hush

Chatur typed it.

"WRONG PASSWORD," the slab boomed.

Chatur tried again.

"ACCOUNT LOCKED. SECURITY BREACH. REPORTING TREASON."

Alarms blared.

Nishachar nodded gravely. "Excellent. System functioning normally."

Lunch Break? Not Quite.

Chatur was starving. The cafeteria menu read:

Today's Options:

- Grass (fresh or stale)
- Random leftovers
- Water if available

As he reached for water, a buffalo blocked his path.

"New employees hydrate LAST."

Chatur stepped back.

"I love dehydration," he said weakly.

End of Onboarding Day 1 (Survival Score: 1/10)

Chatur limped toward the exit, trying to remember why he ever applied.

Just as he reached the gate, Chalu appeared silently from the shadows.

"Rough day?" he asked smoothly.

Chatur exhaled. "A little."

Chalu smiled. “Good. This jungle tests the worthy. Survive the first month… and you may yet thrive.”

Chatur nodded, a spark returning to his eyes.

“I’m not giving up.”

“I know,” Chalu whispered. “That’s why you were hired.”

As Chatur walked away, the wind carried the distant echo of hyenas laughing.

And the jungle whispered back:

Welcome to corporate life, little fox. The real hunt begins tomorrow.

******

Chapter 5
The IT Debacle

If jungles had legends, they would tell stories of Nishachar the Owl—guardian of systems, destroyer of passwords, inventor of security protocols so extreme they made grown tigers weep. Some said he could see cyber-threats before they happened. Others said he just hadn't slept since 1992.

To Chatur, he was simply the architect of trauma.

The morning of Day 2 began innocently enough. Chatur walked into the office determined to redeem himself from the dramatic slip-and-water-barrel incident of the day before. Tail brushed, fur fluffed, optimism dangerously high.

He approached the IT cave again, hoping his stone laptop had stopped screaming.

Nishachar emerged from the shadows like a horror movie jump scare.

"You're late," the owl hooted.

"It's 8:01 again," Chatur said.

Nishachar glared. "IT standard time began at 7:52."

"Why 7:52?" Chatur asked.

"For unpredictability. Hackers can't attack what they can't predict," the owl replied.

Chatur blinked twice, slowly, like a dying battery.

Disaster #1: Password Protocol Apocalypse

"Today," Nishachar announced dramatically, "you must reset your password."

He handed Chatur a leaf containing instructions:

PASSWORD CREATION RULES:

- Minimum 32 characters
- Must include uppercase, lowercase, numbers, symbols, feathers and emotional pain
- Must include at least one existential statement
- No repeating characters allowed
- Must NOT include any word found in any language ever created

Chatur stared. "Emotional pain?"

"Yes. Something unforgettable," the owl said.

After 20 minutes of suffering, Chatur typed:

Ih@teMyLif3AndThisJungl3SoMuch!!

The stone slab responded:

"WEAK. TRY AGAIN."

Chatur tried another:

Pl3a$eL3tM3D!eInPe@ceAndQu!et!

"STILL WEAK."

Third attempt:

WhatEvenIsThePointOfExistenceWhenIDieInsideDaily!?!!#%^&

The slab paused.

Then: **STRONG PASSWORD. ACCEPTED.**

Nishachar nodded approvingly. "Finally, some emotional depth."

Chatur's soul left his body briefly.

Disaster #2: Access Rights

Chatur attempted to open the email system.

ACCESS DENIED – NOT AUTHORIZED

He clicked documents.

ACCESS DENIED – NOT AUTHORIZED

Sales tracker.

ACCESS DENIED – NOT AUTHORIZED

Lunch menu.

ACCESS DENIED – CLASSIFIED

"What AM I authorized to access?" Chatur asked.

Nishachar typed into the system.

The stone tablet displayed:

AUTHORIZED ACCESS: Recycling Bin

"And that too," Nishachar added, "only read-only."

Chatur stared into the void.

Chatu suddenly ran in, panting. "BROTHER! Quick question—did you get access to the CRM?"

"What CRM?" Chatur asked.

Chatu's eyes widened in horror. "OH NO. If Nishachar hasn't granted access by noon, Sales sacrifices a goat!"

Chatur blinked. "A real goat?"

"No, a metaphorical goat," Chatu said. "But last quarter we ran out of metaphors and… it got messy."

Disaster #3: The Antivirus from Hell

Nishachar handed Chatur a floppy mushroom disk labelled **ANTI-VIRUS 2004**.

"This will protect your device," he said.

Chatur inserted it.

The stone laptop shrieked louder than before, emitted a puff of smoke, and displayed:

MALWARE DETECTED: YOUR SYSTEM IS NOW INFECTED

"What did I do?" Chatur yelled.

"You installed protection," Nishachar said calmly. "Sometimes protection is the threat."

The screen began flashing aggressively:

WARNING! DATA LOSS IMMINENT! BACKUP NOW!

Chatur looked around frantically. "Backup where? HOW?"

Nishachar pointed to a wooden drawer full of blank leaves and broken quills.

"That's the backup system," he said.

Chatur felt tears forming.

He began writing his files by hand, furiously scribbling on leaves.

The slab suddenly stopped flashing.

"JUST KIDDING," it displayed. "NO VIRUS."

The owl nodded. "A test to check your resilience."

"I think I blacked out," Chatur whispered.

"Yes," Nishachar said proudly. "Most candidates do."

The Final Blow: Security Audit

Nishachar snapped his wings and announced, "Now, mandatory security check."

He blindfolded Chatur, spun him around ten times, and shouted, "FIND THE EXIT WHILE UNDER THREAT."

Within seconds, alarms blared and Chatur was chased by:

- Three screaming geese
- A malfunctioning printer shooting ink
- A squirrel wielding a stapler

******

Chapter 6
The Great Intro

If there was one thing Junglee Log loved more than meetings, paperwork, and mismanaged expectations, it was **introductions**. The leadership team believed firmly that no employee was officially part of the jungle until they had been publicly displayed, evaluated, applauded, and accidentally humiliated in front of the entire organization.

Today was that day for Chatur.

He arrived early, fur groomed and heart buzzing with anxious energy. Determined to redeem the chaos of onboarding and the IT meltdown, he planned to make this introduction dignified—professional even.

He should have known better.

The Grand Hall Setup

The event was to be held in the **Great Banyan Auditorium**, which was actually an open clearing arranged with tree-stump seating, a termite mound podium, and a suspiciously shaky overhead nest filled with event props. A banner hung in the centre, hand-painted and misspelled as usual:

WELCOME CHATER, OUR NEW SALES AND ACCOUNT MANEGER!

Chatur opened his mouth to correct the spelling, but Chatu the Dog appeared, tail wagging violently.

"BROTHER!! Are you ready for the GREATEST INTRODUCTION OF YOUR LIFE?"

Chatur smiled weakly. "I hope so."

Chatu placed a heavy paw around his shoulder like an affectionate chokehold.

"No pressure, but the entire jungle is here. Leadership expects magic. Marketing expects drama. HR expects tears. And Bolbacchan expects fireworks."

Chatur froze. "Fireworks?"

"Not literal ones!" Chatu barked. "Probably."

The Audience Arrives

Animals poured into the clearing in waves—monkeys swinging like they were late to free bananas, elephants stomping loudly, peacocks strutting, wolves grinning like they smelled emotional blood.

A group of parrots pre-rehearsed synchronized applause.

Two crocodiles sat in the front, sharpening smiles.

And hyenas gathered at the back, drooling laughter.

Bolbacchan flew in circles above everyone shouting:

"MAKE NOISE! SHOW ENERGY! CLAP LIKE YOU MEAN IT!"

Karmat muttered, "All this for free? Unbelievable."

Chakmak glittered aggressively, adjusting feathers every 7 seconds.

Chambu practiced his strategic gaze into the horizon.

And Chalu observed silently from the shadows like an overqualified villain enjoying the coming disaster.

The Show Begins

Chatu bounded onto the stage.

"ANIMALS OF JUNGLEE LOG!! TODAY WE WELCOME A HERO!"

The crowd cheered.

"HE SURVIVED THE INTERVIEW PROCESS!"

More cheering.

"HE SURVIVED ONBOARDING!"

Sympathetic applause.

"AND HE SURVIVED IT SECURITY!"

Gasps. A squirrel fainted.

"PLEASE WELCOME—THE LEGEND—THE VISIONARY—THE FOX—THE ONE WHO SIGNED ALL WAIVERS WITHOUT READING—"

Chatur cringed.

"—MR. CHAAAAAAATUUUUUUR!"

The crowd roared.

Chatur stepped forward, smiling modestly, preparing to speak when—

A monkey from the balcony dropped a banana peel directly under his paw.

Chatur slipped, flipped, spun mid-air, and landed on his back with a thud so dramatic the parrots screamed and the crocodiles clapped.

Chakmak cried joyfully, "WHAT A PERFORMANCE! SO MUCH NATURAL DRAMA!"

Chatu whispered, "Amazing opening, brother! They LOVE you."

Chatur staggered up, soaked in humiliation and leaf debris.

He took a deep breath.

Chatur's Speech

"Thank you," he began. "I'm honoured to join Junglee Log. I look forward to working with all of you and contributing to our expansion and partnerships—"

A branch snapped overhead.

The nest of props fell.

Glitter, leaves, confetti, balloons, and a bucket of honey rained down on him like a theatrical catastrophe.

The monkeys clapped wildly.

Hyenas howled with joy.

Bolbacchan shouted, "THIS IS THE BEST INTRO EVER!"

Chakmak posed dramatically under falling glitter. "THIS IS ART!"

Karmat rubbed his temples. "Expensive art."

Chatu barked, "SHOW THEM YOUR ENERGY, BROTHER! GIVE THEM A LINE THEY'LL REMEMBER!"

Chatur closed his eyes, honey dripping from his ears.

Then he spoke slowly, firmly, surprisingly confidently:

"Success is not about never falling. It's about rising every time, no matter how sticky the floor is."

The jungle went silent.

Then exploded into applause.

Even the hyenas paused.

Even the crocodiles blinked.

Even King Chuha Singh raised an eyebrow in mild respect.

Chalu smirked approvingly.

Chatur bowed awkwardly, sticking slightly to the stage because of the honey.

Post-Event Reactions

The management team gathered backstage.

Chatu beamed. "HE'S A STAR!"

Chakmak fluttered. "WE MUST BRAND HIM! PHOTOSHOOT TOMORROW!"

Bolbacchan screeched, "HE SPEAKS LIKE A POSTER! I LOVE HIM!"

Karmat grumbled, "We need to budget how much glitter we waste daily."

Chambu pondered. "A survivor. Adaptive. Possibly strategic material."

Sunder took notes. "Headline: 'New Fox Rises Despite Sticky Situation.' Sub-headline: 'Performance Leaves Audience Glued to Seats.'"

Nishachar hooted suspiciously. “We shall see how he handles access requests tomorrow.”

And Chalu simply whispered:

“He learns fast. Good. Very good.”

******

Chapter 7
The Chatu Effect

Power in Junglee Log didn't flow through official titles, organizational charts, or strategy documents. Those were decorations—like feathers on a peacock or disclaimers on an insurance form. The true source of power, the one force feared, admired, whispered about, and occasionally sacrificed bananas to, was **Chatu**.

Chatu the Dog – Chief of Staff, King Chuha Singh's shadow, cheerleader, translator, emotional support animal, and unofficial Minister of Threats.

He was everywhere. Always wagging, always smiling, always saying "Yes, My King" with such enthusiasm that the trees shook. But beneath that wagging tail was a sharp political weapon. And every creature in Junglee Log knew one universal truth:

If you pleased Chatu, you survived. If you crossed him, you vanished.

Chatur learned this the hard way – very quickly.

The Warning Begins

The morning after his grand introduction performance, Chatur was walking through the office clearing, still sticky with dried honey and glitter, when a nervous rabbit hopped up beside him.

"Congratulations on surviving your intro," the rabbit said timidly. "And um... word of advice. Whatever you do... don't get on the wrong side of Chatu."

Chatur blinked. "Chatu? But he seems nice. Very enthusiastic. Very supportive."

The rabbit shivered like someone had poured ice water on his spine.

"That's how it starts."

Before Chatur could ask more, the rabbit bolted away as if chased by fate itself.

Moments later, a buffalo passing by muttered, "May the jungle protect you, kid," like someone praying for the dead.

Chatur felt confused.

Then a lemur leaned in and whispered urgently, "If he smiles too much, run."

A porcupine added, "If he says you're his favourite, write your will."

Chatur stood frozen as animals dispersed like someone had dropped a predator in the cafeteria.

The Legend of the Chatu Effect

Finally, an old tortoise approached. Slow, calm, and carrying the weight of a thousand HR disputes.

"I heard you're the new fox," the tortoise croaked.

"Yes, sir," Chatur said respectfully.

The tortoise nodded. "Good. Listen carefully. There's something you need to understand if you plan to survive here."

He cleared his throat dramatically.

"Years ago, there was an eagle named Tej. Brilliant. Sharp. Independent thinker. The king loved him... for about ten minutes."

"What happened?" Chatur asked.

"Tej disagreed with Chatu in a meeting. Publicly." The tortoise shuddered. "By the next day, all communication labelled him as 'toxic influence'. HR launched a 'culture investigation.' His desk was moved next to the restroom. His projects vanished. And eventually..."

The tortoise looked upward meaningfully.

"...he flew away. Forever."

Before Chatur could process, a meerkat popped out of the ground.

"You think that's bad? There was a zebra named Reshma. She suggested the king should speak less and listen more."

Chatur winced. "That sounds reasonable."

"So did her funeral speech," the meerkat whispered.

"And then there was Jaggu the Jackal," a hyena chimed in, appearing from nowhere. "Tried to give performance feedback to Chatu."

"What happened?"

The hyena leaned close.

"No one knows. He just... disappeared. Some say he transferred to another jungle. Others say..."

The hyena's grin widened.

"...his bones are buried under the conference platform."

Chatur's fur stood on end.

Chatu Appears

As if summoned by the fear floating in the air, Chatu bounded into the clearing.

"BROTHER FOX!!" he barked joyfully, crushing Chatur into a rib-crunching hug.

The surrounding animals flinched.

"How is your second day going?" Chatu asked, tail wagging violently.

"Great!" Chatur managed to choke out.

"AMAZING!" Chatu beamed. "Just remember – if you ever need anything, ANYTHING at all, come to me. I'll take care of it. Always."

Animals nearby exchanged looks of horror.

Chatur smiled weakly, trying not to stop breathing.

"I'm lucky to have your support," he said.

Chatu's eyes gleamed.

"YES. Loyalty is EVERYTHING in Junglee Log."

Then he trotted away, humming a cheerful tune completely at odds with the palpable fear in the air.

The Truth Unveiled

Once Chatu was gone, animals deflated like someone had stepped off their chest.

A small sparrow fluttered close.

"That," she whispered, "is the **Chatu Effect**. When he's around – everyone smiles. When he's gone – everyone survives."

A goat nodded solemnly. "If he likes you, he'll protect you. If he doesn't, he'll destroy you. And the king will never know because Chatu controls information."

A raccoon added, "He decides who sits where. Who gets promoted. Who gets blamed. Who gets thrown under the bus. Who gets fed to wolves."

"Wolves?" Chatur gulped.

The raccoon nodded. "Metaphorically. Mostly."

The old tortoise tapped Chatur's paw.

"So be smart. Be polite. Never contradict him. Never outperform him publicly. And above all – never forget this lesson."

Chatur leaned in.

The tortoise whispered:

"In Junglee Log, the king rules the jungle – but Chatu rules the king."

A chill travelled down Chatur's spine.

For the first time since joining, he felt something stronger than anxiety.

He felt **danger**.

Chalu Watches

From across the clearing, the Silver Fox observed silently. Tail still, eyes sharp, smile unreadable.

He saw fear spreading.

He saw loyalties shifting.

He saw Chatur realizing the truth.

And he whispered to himself:

"The real game begins now."

******

Chapter 8
The Parrot Parody

If noise had a physical form, it would be Bolbacchan the Parrot. Head of Sales. Chief Echo Specialist. Professional Loudmouth. Creature capable of turning silence into chaos within three seconds.

In Junglee Log, his voice was more powerful than logic, facts, budgets, or any actual sales numbers. The common joke was:

"If Bolbacchan says it louder, it becomes true."

Sales meetings felt less like planning discussions and more like rock concerts without instruments – just pure verbal assault.

Today, Chatur was about to experience his **first Sales War Room**.

And nothing could have prepared him.

The Sales Den

Deep inside the jungle stood a cave decorated with broken flipcharts, half-eaten fruit baskets, motivational posters that contradicted each other, and a giant gong used for reasons no one fully understood.

Bolbacchan stood at the centre of the chaos, pacing like a general preparing for battle.

"TEAM!" he screeched at a decibel level that caused birds in a neighbouring jungle to migrate early. "TODAY WE TALK STRATEGY!"

A pigeon fainted.

A deer clamped its hooves over its ears.

A lizard fell off the ceiling.

Chatur sat nervously beside a warthog who leaned in and whispered:

"Rule one: Do NOT question him. Rule two: Do NOT interrupt him. Rule three: If you value your hearing, sit near the exit."

Before Chatur could respond, Bolbacchan slapped a massive chart onto the wall.

The chart contained arrows, doodles, and the word **TARGET** written 17 times in different colors, sizes, and levels of desperation.

Bolbacchan flapped his wings violently.

"WE NEED NUMBERS! WE NEED RESULTS! WE NEED VICTORY!"

"What are our current numbers?" a duck asked timidly.

Bolbacchan froze, eyes bulging.

"IRRELEVANT!" he shrieked. "WE MUST VISUALIZE SUCCESS!"

He grabbed the gong mallet and struck it.

The entire cave vibrated.

Sales motivation had begun.

The Parrot Pitching Method

Bolbacchan puffed up his feathers dramatically.

"Chatur! NEW FOX! FRONT AND CENTER!"

Chatur stood, heart pounding.

"Today," Bolbacchan declared, "you learn the sacred art of SALES."

He pointed to a board with the official **Parrot Sales Methodology** written in glitter:

1. **Say it Loud**
2. **Say it Again**
3. **Say it Louder**
4. **If they disagree, scream until they surrender**

Chatur blinked. "Isn't there space for listening to the client?"

Bolbacchan stared in horror.

"LISTENING?" he screeched. "THIS IS SALES, NOT SCIENCE!"

He turned dramatically to the group.

"WHAT DO WE DO WHEN A CLIENT SAYS NO?"

The team shouted in unison:

"WE SPEAK LOUDER!"

Chatur swallowed fear.

Live-Action Roleplay: The Client Meeting Simulation

Bolbacchan dragged Chatur to the front.

"You are the salesperson! I am the client!" he announced.

He immediately transformed his expression into one of furious scepticism.

"WHY SHOULD I JOIN JUNGLEE LOG?" he screamed.

Chatur took a breath. "Because we offer partnership, growth, and community—"

"NO!" Bolbacchan roared.

Chatur tried again, louder. "Because we can help you expand—"

"NO!"

Chatur raised his voice. "Because our ecosystem—"

"NO NO NO!"

The warthog nudged Chatur. *"Say something ridiculous. He loves drama."*

Chatur inhaled deeply.

"BECAUSE WE WILL PERSONALLY ESCORT YOUR CHILDREN TO SCHOOL DURING MONSOONS!"

Bolbacchan froze.

Then burst into applause.

"YES! YES! EMOTIONAL MANIPULATION! BEAUTIFUL!"

The sales team cheered like a stadium crowd.

A monkey began chanting, "CHA-TUR! CHA-TUR! CHA-TUR!"

Chatur stood there in shock, half-proud, half-concerned for his morals.

The Truth Behind the Screech

During a break, Chatur sat in a corner catching his breath.

A tortoise wearing thick earmuffs rolled over.

"Don't look so surprised," he said. "Bolbacchan has been doing this for years. His voice can convince anyone of anything. Last year he talked a lion into buying his own tail back."

A rabbit nodded. "And he once convinced Finance that a deficit was actually a surplus because he explained it loudly enough."

A pigeon added, "His strategy deck has zero data. But it has 47 slides of him screaming the word GROWTH."

Chatur exhaled. "So he's successful because he's loud?"

The tortoise chuckled. "No. Because the king loves passion more than logic. And Bolbacchan gives passion like a firework launched indoors."

Chatur nodded slowly.

Another voice whispered behind him.

It was Chalu.

"Remember this lesson, little fox," he murmured. "In Junglee Log, sales isn't about truth. It's about volume."

Chatur turned to him. "That sounds dangerous."

Chalu smiled thinly. "Oh, it is. And one day, that noise will explode. Make sure you're not holding the match."

Then he vanished back into the crowd.

Bolbacchan's Final Announcement

Bolbacchan banged the gong again, startling everyone back into silence.

"TEAM! NEXT WEEK WE LAUNCH A SALES TOUR ACROSS JUNGLES!" he declared. "WE WILL CONQUER THE MARKET AND MAKE HISTORY!"

Everyone clapped like their salaries depended on it – because they did.

"Chatur," the parrot screeched joyfully, "you are coming with me! FRONTLINE SALES!"

Chatur froze.

Frontline?

In hostile jungles?

With Bolbacchan screaming beside him?

He felt his spirit attempt to exit his body.

But he smiled anyway.

"Of course," he said.

Bolbacchan grinned like a creature unhinged.

"BRING EARPLUGS!" the warthog whispered.

******

Chapter 9
Into the Battlefield - Client Prospecting Pandemonium

No amount of onboarding, motivational screaming, or glitter showers could have prepared Chatur for his first real day in the wild world of **client prospecting**. If sales meetings were chaotic, client visits were warfare disguised as hospitality.

Bolbacchan the Parrot dragged Chatur through the jungle at lightning speed, wings flapping, excitement radiating like unstable dynamite.

"TODAY, LITTLE FOX, WE HUNT!" he screeched.

Chatur panted behind him, clutching a folder of brochures. "We're… hunting prospects?"

"HUNTING CONTRACTS!" Bolbacchan corrected. "CLIENTS ARE PREY! OPPORTUNITY IS MEAT! TARGETS ARE BLOOD!"

Chatur slowed down. "…Should we maybe use different metaphors when talking to the herbivores?"

Bolbacchan gasped. "HERESY! PASSION HAS NO METAPHOR LIMITS!"

Chatur mentally wrote this down next to: *Never suggest alternatives to Bolbacchan unless wearing protective gear.*

Client #1: The Deer Corporation

They arrived at a clearing populated by deer wearing tiny glasses and holding leaf notebooks.

"Welcome to DeerSoft Technologies," their leader said gently. "We value peace, harmony, and quiet collaborative spaces."

Bolbacchan inhaled deeply — always a bad sign.

"HELLOOOOOOO!!! WE ARE HERE TO SELL YOU THE FUTURE!" he screamed.

Fifteen deer fainted.

One managed to squeak, "Inside voices please?"

Bolbacchan ignored them. "JUNGLEE LOG WILL TRANSFORM YOUR WORLD! JOIN US FOR GROWTH, SYNERGY, AND UNLIMITED OPPORTUNITY!"

Chatur leaned forward politely. "What are some of your current challenges?"

A trembling deer replied, "Mostly avoiding heart attacks."

Bolbacchan slammed his wing onto a rock like a judge delivering a death sentence.

"WE WILL FIX THAT! WE PROVIDE STABILITY! SECURITY! STRUCTURE!"

The rock shattered.

The deer scattered.

Bolbacchan turned to Chatur, feathers smoking slightly.

"EXCELLENT MEETING! THEY LOVE US!"

Chatur stared at the empty clearing. "...Do they?"

"NEGOTIATIONS HAVE BEGUN!" Bolbacchan declared triumphantly.

Negotiations, apparently, meant *everyone running for their lives.*

Client #2: The Bear Consortium

Next, they approached a cave decorated with honey jars and warning signs reading **DO NOT ANGER US BEFORE BREAKFAST**.

Bolbacchan marched straight in.

"GREETINGS, FURRY PARTNERS! LET'S TALK BUSINESS!"

A massive bear growled, "Do you have an appointment?"

Bolbacchan beamed. "APPOINTMENT IS A HUMAN CONCEPT! WE HAVE DESTINY!"

The bears looked seconds away from ripping destiny limb from limb.

Chatur jumped forward.

"We bring an opportunity for mutual benefit," he said carefully. "A model where resources and support flow both ways."

A bear paused. "Mutual growth?"

"Yes!" Chatur said. "With specific structure, timelines, and shared governance."

Bolbacchan interrupted. "AND FREE HONEY FOR EVERYONE!"

Chatur's head snapped toward him. *There was no honey program.*

The bears gasped. "Free… honey?"

Bolbacchan nodded furiously. "YES! UNLIMITED!! PURE ORGANIC CERTIFIED BY OWLS!!"

Chatur whispered urgently, "We don't have honey."

Bolbacchan whispered back, "We will figure it out. Finance will cry. It is tradition."

The bears lifted Bolbacchan into the air cheering.

Chatur sighed.

Client #3: The Hyena Coalition

Prospecting rules #1–#999: NEVER approach laughing predators.

Bolbacchan, of course, did.

"HELLO HYENAS! LET'S DISCUSS STRATEGIC PARTNERSH—"

The hyenas burst into hysterical laughter before he finished speaking.

"What's funny?" Chatur asked cautiously.

One hyena wiped tears. "You think YOU can manage US?"

Another cackled, "We eat strategy for breakfast and spit out PowerPoints."

Bolbacchan puffed up confidently. "WE OFFER EXCELLENCE! ORGANIZATION! PROCESS!"

The hyenas howled.

"Organization? You can't organize your eyebrows!"

Bolbacchan squawked defensively. "MY EYEBROWS ARE A SYMBOL OF PASSION!"

Chatur stepped in.

"We understand your concerns. Maybe instead of managing, we could collaborate based on autonomy?"

The hyenas paused, confused.

One scratched his head. "What does that mean?"

Chatur smiled. "Basically – you do what you want, and we support you."

The hyenas grinned. "Now THAT'S partnership!"

Bolbacchan threw his wings in the air. "SUCCESS! WE ARE GENIUSES!"

Chatur pinched the bridge of his nose.

Post-Prospecting Debrief

On the way back, Bolbacchan flew dramatically in circles.

"WHAT A DAY! WHAT MOMENTUM! WHAT SALES ENERGY!"

Chatur dragged his feet. "We nearly got murdered three times."

Bolbacchan nodded proudly. "YES! THE SIGN OF EFFECTIVE PROSPECTING!!"

"Is there a metric for how many clients faint?" Chatur asked.

"YES," Bolbacchan said. "Fainting indicates emotional engagement."

Chatur stared at him, unsure whether to laugh or flee.

"Rest well, little fox," Bolbacchan said. "Tomorrow – follow-up calls!"

Chatur felt his soul leave his body.

Chalu Observes Again

From a treetop, Chalu watched.

He smirked.

"Thrown into battle with madness on one side and predators on the other..."

He whispered:

"Let's see if you survive, young fox."

******

Chapter 10
Client Chronicles - Chaos, Commitments & Catastrophe

If **prospecting** was a battlefield, then **client servicing** was trenching warfare — with flaming arrows, broken walkie-talkies, and commanders giving contradictory orders while pretending everything was under control.

After the infamous honey-promise tour, Junglee Log was buzzing louder than Bolbacchan on caffeine. Word had spread across jungles far and wide:

Junglee Log is expanding. Bears are crying. Hyenas are laughing. Deer are traumatized.

And every jungle now wanted to see whether Chatur — the new fox whose reputation was now defined as *the guy who got hugged by bears and survived* — could live up to the hype.

By sunrise, Chatur's workload had multiplied like monkeys in mating season.

He walked into the headquarters ready for a calm day.

Naturally, that was delusion.

Morning Shockwave: The Follow-Up Frenzy

Chatur entered the office to find Bolbacchan standing on a desk screaming instructions while holding three leaf-phones at once.

"FOLLOW-UPS! FOLLOW-UPS! FOLLOW-UPS!" he shrieked. "NO PROSPECT LEFT ALIVE – I MEAN, UNCALLED!"

Chatur froze.

The Sales team looked like soldiers after a storm – eyes hollow, hair missing, a warthog clutching a stress leaf like a rosary.

A buffalo whispered to Chatur, "Coffee ran out. Paramedics on standby. Save yourself."

Chatur sat down and dialled the first number.

A deer answered nervously, "DeerSoft support, how may I assist you?"

Chatur smiled politely. "Hello! Following up regarding our partnership discussion—"

The deer screamed, "NO NO NO PLEASE NO SCREAMING TODAY WE'RE STILL RECOVERING!" and hung up

Chatur stared at the phone.

Bolbacchan beamed. "Excellent! Strong interest!"

Call #2: The Bears Demand Blood Sugar

The next call connected to the Bear Consortium.

"Hello," Chatur said carefully.

The lead bear growled cheerfully, "WHEN IS THE HONEY ARRIVING? OUR CHILDREN HAVE CLEANED THE TABLES FOR THE GRAND FEAST!"

Chatur gulped. "We're finalizing logistics—"

"DO YOU REQUIRE OUR HELP TO CARRY THE TRUCKS?" the bear offered.

"There are no trucks," Chatur whispered.

Silence.

Then a dangerous rumble.

"NO TRUCKS? WHAT IS THE MEANING OF THIS?"

Bolbacchan grabbed the phone and shrieked, "WE ARE CREATING CUSTOM GOLD-LABEL HONEY PACKAGING! DELAY IS FOR PERFECTION!"

The bears gasped adoringly. "PERFECTION! WE WAIT WITH HONOR!"

Chatur mouthed silently, *We're all going to die.*

Call #3: The Hyenas Negotiate

The hyenas answered mid-laughter.

"Fox! We like fox! Fox talks good!" the lead hyena cackled.

Chatur smiled. "Glad to hear! We'd like to schedule a partnership alignment call—"

The hyenas exploded into laughter again.

A hyena shouted, "Align what?? Our vertebrae?"

Another wheezed, "Call tomorrow? No tomorrow! Tomorrow might explode!"

"Everything explodes eventually!" another yelled.

Chatur blinked. "So… is that a yes?"

"YES! NO! MAYBE! WE DECIDE WHEN THE MOON SCREAMS!"

Click.

Chatur stared at the receiver.

Bolbacchan punched the air. "THAT'S A STRONG LEAD!"

Chatur whispered, "That's a medical emergency."

Behind-the-Scenes Panic

Meanwhile, behind closed leaves, chaos brewed.

In Finance, Karmat stomped down the hallway, yelling:

"WHO SIGNED A PURCHASE ORDER FOR FOUR THOUSAND LITERS OF HONEY?? THAT'S MORE THAN THE AMOUNT PRODUCED IN THIS HEMISPHERE IN A YEAR!"

Balwaan from HR squeaked, "The bears asked for honey insurance! They want emotional coverage in case expectations aren't met! WHAT IS EMOTIONAL COVERAGE??"

Sunder from Comms burst in waving a draft press note.

"Headline: *Junglee Log Innovates Sweet Partnership Model!* Sub-headline: *Sticky But Strategic!*"

Karmat stared at him like a rhino ready to charge.

"Are you mocking my suffering?"

"No," Sunder said proudly. "I'm monetizing it."

In Marketing, Chakmak yelled, "PHOTO SHOOT AT SUNSET WITH HONEY BUCKET BACKDROPS! EVERYONE SHINE! GLITTER CANNONS ON STANDBY!"

Monkeys unpacked confetti cannons labelled *EMERGENCY BRANDING.*

The IT cave flickered red.

Nishachar appeared, feathers ruffled, pupils dilated.

"NO ONE IS ALLOWED TO DOWNLOAD HONEY FILES!" he screamed.

Everyone froze.

"WHAT IS A HONEY FILE??" Karmat yelled.

"I DON'T KNOW BUT SOMEONE TRIED AND THE SERVERS HAD A BREAKDOWN," Nishachar hooted.

"Does the server store honey?" a squirrel asked.

Nishachar hissed, "ASK THAT AGAIN AND I WILL DELETE YOUR EXISTENCE."

Escalation Meeting of Doom

Chatur was summoned to an emergency leadership meeting.

He sat at the centre like a defendant awaiting sentencing.

Chakmak opened dramatically. "WE HAVE A CRISIS. THE WORLD EXPECTS HONEY."

Karmat slammed a ledger. "WE HAVE ZERO HONEY."

Sunder cleared his throat. "The bears tweeted about us."

Everyone gasped.

He read aloud:

The sweet revolution begins. #HoneyOrHonor #JungleeLogForever

Chatu barked proudly, "POSITIVE SENTIMENT!"

"POSITIVE??" Karmat roared. "IF WE FAIL, THEY WILL EAT US!"

Chalu finally spoke.

"Let the fox talk."

The room fell silent.

All eyes turned to Chatur.

He swallowed.

"The problem is not honey," he said slowly. "The problem is expectation management. We need alignment, not sugar."

Blank stares.

He continued.

"If we turn this into a joint venture – resource pooling, collaborative production, shared marketing – we make bears part of the solution. And eliminate blame."

Chakmak gasped. "BRILLIANT! BRAND STORYLINE: *MADE TOGETHER!*"

Sunder wrote furiously. "Headlines: Bears & Junglee Log Co-Create Sweet Success!"

Karmat grunted. "That costs less. I approve."

Chatu bark-cheered. "FOX IS A GENIUS!"

Chalu smiled without smiling.

"Good move, young fox," he murmured.

The Follow-Up Firestorm

Chatur and Bolbacchan began joint calls.

DeerSoft answered still trembling.

Chatur spoke gently. "We'd love to rebuild a calm, mutually beneficial conversation."

Bolbacchan whispered,

"SHOULD I SCREAM?"

"No," Chatur said firmly.

The deer sighed in relief.

Meanwhile, the bears roared happily about collaboration, and hyenas laughed for several hours straight without reason.

Result:

- DeerSoft booked a pilot discussion
- Bear Consortium agreed to honey co-production
- Hyenas promised partnership *when the moon screams*

Bolbacchan burst into tears.

"FOX! WE DID IT! MY HEART IS SWEATING WITH JOY!"

Chatur blinked. "He means beating fast…"

"No," the buffalo whispered. "His heart literally sweats. Medical anomaly."

Evening Reflections

Chatur finally left the office at dusk.

His body ached. His mind throbbed. His soul whimpered.

But he felt something new.

Confidence.

Not comfort — that didn't exist here.

But the realization he might actually survive.

As he walked out, Chalu appeared from the shadows.

“Well done,” he said softly. “You turned madness into momentum.”

Chatur exhaled. “Thank you.”

Chalu’s smile sharpened.

“Careful, fox. With success comes visibility. And visibility attracts hunters.”

Chatur stiffened.

“Are you warning me?”

“No,” Chalu said. “I’m welcoming you to the game.”

Chatur watched him disappear into the darkness.

And the jungle whispered:

Survive today. Fight tomorrow.

******

Chapter 11
The Silver Fox

In most civilized ecosystems, corporate hierarchy is drawn as a tidy pyramid. In Junglee Log, however, hierarchy resembled a tangled cluster of vines, duct-taped to a termite mound, occasionally set on fire for entertainment. Titles existed, yes — but actual power moved according to whisper networks, selective alliances, glitter consumption ratios, and emotional blackmail.

And in this ecosystem sat **Chalu**, the Silver Fox — Senior Business Manager, master strategist, King Chuha Singh's original golden prodigy, and the most politically dangerous animal within four jungles.

Everyone respected him. Everyone feared him. Everyone wanted to know what moisturizer made his fur shine like moonlight.

For years, he had been the rising star — the unchallenged crown prince, the genius nobody dared compete with.

Until a new fox appeared.

Chatur.

The unexpected success of the Honey Crisis had changed everything. Suddenly, Chatur was being spoken about — not as the new recruit, not as the clueless intern-like employee who tripped into barrels and survived IT torture

– but as someone with potential. Someone who delivered. Someone who didn't crumble under chaos.

And that, in Junglee Log, was offensive.

Never outshine the star. Never survive where you're expected to fail. Never accidentally become competent.

But Chatur had.

And now the Silver Fox was watching.

The Shift in Atmosphere

The morning after the successful client calls, Chatur walked into the clearing outside HQ and instantly sensed something was different.

Animals stopped mid-conversation. Whispering spread like wind.

A buffalo stared at him like he'd seen a ghost. A monkey dropped an entire bunch of bananas on his own foot. A squirrel fainted dramatically.

"Wow," Chatur thought. "All this because I attended three meetings?"

Before he could make sense of it, Chatu bounded toward him like a sugar-fuelled rocket.

"BROTHER FOX!!! YOU ARE A LEGEND!!! THE KING SAID YOUR NAME WITHOUT HESITATION!"

Chatur blinked. "Is that… rare?"

The buffalo leaned in and whispered, "He still calls his wife 'Hey You.'"

Chatur swallowed.

A group of monkeys began chanting quietly, "Fuuuuuture leaaaaaader," like a creepy sports crowd.

And then the crowd parted.

The Silver Fox arrived.

Chalu walked with the silent grace of a seasoned predator – the kind who smiled while calculating exactly how to dismantle your life.

"Congratulations, Chatur," Chalu said softly, with a smile that felt colder than night. "Not many survive their first crisis here. Fewer still turn it around."

Chatur offered a polite nod. "Thank you. It was a team effort."

Chalu's eyes flicked, amused.

"Of course it was," he said. "But let's not pretend results don't have owners."

Then he leaned closer.

"Just remember – nothing spreads faster than success. And nothing threatens stability more than change."

Chatur wasn't sure whether to feel flattered or terrified.

Probably both.

The Meeting of Sharp Smiles

Later, Chatur received a cryptic summon:

MANDATORY LEADERSHIP HUDDLE - BE ON TIME OR FACE UNKNOWN CONSEQUENCES

He followed the trail of wooden signboards (some upside down) until he reached the Grand Banyan Conference Circle.

Inside sat:

- **King Chuha Singh**, radiating royal impatience
- **Chalu**, looking calm like a villain who studied meditation for aesthetic purposes
- **Chatu**, vibrating with excitement
- **Bolbacchan**, rehearsing screaming silently
- **Chakmak**, fixing feathers aggressively
- **Karmat**, looking like he regretted existence
- **Sunder**, armed with press notes
- **Nishachar**, scanning everyone for suspected treason
- **Balwaan**, sweating like responsibility itself

Chuha Singh growled, "We need rapid expansion. Which means execution excellence. Which means accountability. Which means assigning critical ownership."

Everyone nodded dramatically.

Chalu stood.

"With the new momentum around Bear Consortium, DeerSoft Technologies, and the Hyena Coalition, we need strong leadership. I propose we appoint Chatur as *Strategic Account Lead* for all three initiatives."

Chatur nearly choked.

It was a massive responsibility. It was an opportunity. It was also a tactical death trap.

Chatu burst into applause like a seal learning tricks.

"YES! BROTHER IS READY FOR GLORY!"

Bolbacchan screamed, "WE BELIEVE!!!" loud enough to crack a termite mound.

Chakmak flung glitter into the air.

Nishachar muttered, "He will beg for mercy soon."

Karmat whispered, "We are so doomed."

Sunder scribbled headline ideas: *"FOX LEADS FUTURE" / "FAILURE IMMINENT?"*

Chuha Singh nodded. "Approved. Let the fox lead."

Everyone clapped while making the faces of people watching a slow-motion train crash.

Chatur sat there smiling like someone pretending to enjoy being stabbed politely.

Chalu sat back, satisfied.

The trap was set.

The Politics Begins

The moment Chatur stepped out of the meeting, the lobby exploded with rumors.

"Did you hear? Chatur is taking over key accounts!"

"Chalu must be furious."

"No way – Chalu *suggested* it."

"Exactly. That means something bad is coming."

"We should buy emotional insurance."

A lemur whispered, "Better update your wills."

Chatur exhaled. "Is everyone always this dramatic?"

The buffalo sighed. "You haven't seen anything yet."

Invisible Punches

Within two hours:

- Chatur's meeting room booking disappeared
- His laptop access reset itself to **RECYCLING BIN ONLY**
- Documents needed for planning mysteriously vanished
- Someone switched his ergonomic log seat with a miniature one sized for a squirrel
- The projector began showing only cat videos
- His pen screamed when he clicked it

Bolbacchan tried to fix the projector by yelling "FOCUS!!!" at it.

It remained unfocused.

The warthog offered sympathy. "Initiation rites. Happens to everyone who rises."

"Did it happen to you?" Chatur asked.

"No," the warthog said. "I never rose."

Chatur Fights Back (Accidentally)

With no access to tools, presentation resources, or emotional stability, Chatur did the unthinkable.

He improvised.

The planning call began with the Bear Consortium.

The projector malfunctioned.

The call bridge crashed.

Bolbacchan inhaled preparing to scream.

Chatur raised a paw.

"No visuals. No slides. Just conversation. Real talk."

The bears paused.

Then nodded.

"Impressive. No nonsense. We like."

Meeting success score: **1–0.**

Then came DeerSoft.

Chatur began gently, "No raised voices. Let's build trust first."

The deer relaxed visibly and agreed to a pilot workshop.

Meeting success score: **2–0.**

Then the hyenas.

They laughed for seven continuous minutes.

Finally one yelled, "FOX SPEAKS TRUTH. WE WILL JOIN YOUR CHAOS PARADE!"

Meeting success score: **3–0.**

The Sales War Room erupted into screaming applause.

Bolbacchan sobbed dramatically.

"YOU ARE A LEGEND! MY HEART IS SWEATING BLOOD!"

The buffalo whispered, "That's not healthy."

Chatur smiled weakly.

Whispers of Power Shift

By late afternoon, the whispers changed tone:

"Chatur is not dying. He is winning."

"Chalu looked irritated."

"Is the young fox the next successor?"

"Should we update our loyalties?"

"Will there be snacks?"

Even the hyenas sent a congratulatory fruit basket (mostly half-eaten).

The Silver Fox Strikes Back

As Chatur packed up to leave, he felt a cold breeze.

Chalu appeared behind him without sound – like a haunting.

"Well played today," Chalu said softly. "You handled chaos with grace. That's rare."

"Thank you," Chatur replied cautiously.

Chalu stepped closer.

"But understand something. In this jungle, success is an invitation. An invitation to attention. To envy. To conflict. The higher you climb, the colder the air gets."

Chatur held his gaze. "I'm not trying to climb. I'm just trying to do good work."

Chalu smiled – politely, beautifully, terrifyingly.

"That's exactly what makes you dangerous."

He stepped back.

"The game has begun, young fox. I hope you know how to play."

Then he walked away, his silver tail slicing through the air like a blade.

Chatur stood frozen.

Finally understanding:

This wasn't an opportunity. It was a war.

******

Chapter 12
To Greener Pastures

Silver Fox was not loud. He did not roar like the Lion, nor bark orders like the Bulldog . He simply smiled. A thin, polite smile—the kind that made others shiver more than an open threat would.

One morning, staring through his cabin glass at Chatur who was briefing two interns with hand gestures appropriate for a Bollywood action film, Silver Fox whispered to himself:

"Ah, Chatur… my chatty friend. You've mistaken noise for power.

Let the games begin.".

Goal 1: "Convert Chatur from "Hot Star" → "Warm Leftover."

Strategy: Remove Chatur from decision-making without removing him physically.

The very next week, invitations to important leadership meetings mysteriously began arriving **five minutes after those meetings ended**.

Chatur would walk into Silver Fox's cabin breathless, sweating, holding his phone like a battle shield.

"Hi! I didn't receive the link for the strategic alignment meeting! Must be a mail server glitch?"

Silver Fox widened his eyes innocently—Oscar-worthy performance:

"Oh dear, that's terrible. Technology can be so unreliable. Did you check your Spam folder?" he continued "Don't worry I already covered for you in the meeting. Told everyone you were unwell and running late" he said slyly trying to hide his shrewd face.

"Well," Silver Fox said sympathetically, patting him like a mildly useful house pet, "don't worry. I'll update you about the meeting later."

Later never came.

Only PowerPoint slides came to him—carefully designed so that no meaningful information existed in them. One slide even had a large photo of a cat typing on a keyboard under the title *"Synergy."*

After such repeated missed meetings and core discussion by Chatur, the management gradually began associating **"important work"** with Silver Fox and **"irrelevant recaps"** with Chatur. Little did they know that the outward **"Supporting"** team mate of Chatur was in fact framing his professional character assassination.

Phase 2 – Deployment to Mundanistan

Strategy: Keep Chatur busy with meaningless tasks until he forgets what sunlight looks like.

One Friday afternoon, Silver Fox summoned Chatur with the tone used to announce a national emergency.

"Chatur, this is critical. We need to plan a detailed hour by hour itinerary for the upcoming sales Offsite, from sessions to food menu everything needs to be perfect. Chatu has suggested you handle this responsibility personally. Will help you showcase your organisational skills."

"Offsite Planning?", quipped Chatur, "isn't it something Balwaan and his team should be doing?"

"Come On Chatur, what is wrong with you. You are the future sales leader of Junglee Log, lets show them you are beyond sales calls and ready for the next step. Take Ownership" said Chalu, Silver fox, trying to hide is giggle.

Chatur blinked. Twice. But said nothing.

He spent next 3 three days planning meticulously for the event like it was his wedding.

He created a 62-page report titled **"Sales and Leadership Summit: Road Map to the future"**. He created heat-maps, location and amenities swot and travel cost estimates.

He presented the report proudly in the weekly leadership forum.

The room exploded with laughter.

BolBaccha seemed embarrassed. Karmat sighed. Chalu watched silently as his plan worked perfectly.

Chuha Singh was furious. "Chatur, you are such a disappointment. Here I was thinking of you as a matured and diligent employee and here you are presenting me a report on a "Offsite", I am really disappointed in you."

"This is ridiculous", joined in Chatu.

"I think we are being too hard on Chatur. Afterall he is too young to understand responsibilities. It's natural at his age an offsite excites him." Dropped in Chalu. He continued "We should appreciate the sincerity in his efforts."

Chatur was stunned. He was staring jaw dropped at Chalu as words seemed to drop of his mouth. He knew that moment he had walked right into the trap.

"Now this is what I call maturity; you are blessed to have such a senior colleague who support you like that Chatur" said Chuha Singh with admiration towards Chalu.

Phase 3 Reputation Erosion via Friendly Fire

Strategy: Make Chatur appear like a well-meaning disaster.

Silver Fox began forwarding every minor client issue to Chatur:

For each item Chatur responded with seriousness usually reserved for hostage negotiations.

He would storm around like an ambulance siren, wearing his "Problem Solver" badge, shouting instructions to no one in particular.

Meanwhile, real corporate decisions—strategy, product roadmaps, partnership negotiations—happened quietly in closed rooms.

Where was Chatur? Giving cold call training to interns!

Slowly but surely the management was changing their opinion of Chatur. From the blue-eyed boy to one time wonder—the shift in perception was shaping up rapidly.

The Meeting Marathon Punishment

Chatur's calendar mutated like a radioactive spreadsheet.

He was booked into:

- *Emergency Follow-Up of Yesterday's Follow-Up*
- *Meeting to Finalize the Scheduling of Future Meetings*
- *Brainstorming on Why Brainstorming Isn't Working*
- *Quick Sync (5 hours)*

In one infamous meeting, the outcome was a unanimous decision to schedule another meeting.

Bolbacchan announced:

"PASSION WAS LOW! WE RETAKE TOMORROW WITH SCREAMING!"

Three animals fainted from emotional dehydration.

The Performance Review Execution Ritual

The final straw arrived during the Performance Review Council – an annual ritual where employees were emotionally disembowelled for sport.

Chatur stood in the spotlight, surrounded by solemn judges.

Chalu began:

"Chatur, your results are promising. But there are concerns about cultural alignment."

Chatur blinked. "Cultural alignment?"

Chakmak flared his feathers. "You don't sparkle. You don't glitter. It's dangerous."

Bolbacchan shrieked, "ALSO YOU DO NOT SCREAM! YOU SPEAK LIKE A TEACHER!!!"

Nishachar hooted, "Your password contains no self-loathing. Suspicious."

Karmat rumbled, "You ask where the budget goes. That threatens the natural order."

Sunder read solemnly, "Public perception: you are nice. This damages morale."

Chatu barked passionately, "BUT HE HAS SOUL!"

Everyone recoiled like he'd confessed to loving poetry.

Chalu delivered the fatal blow like a surgeon of destruction:

"Empathy is weakness. Leaders without spine crumble. You hesitate. That makes you unfit for war."

A hyena in the back wiped tears. "Don't worry, we all start with souls. Then we grind them into dust."

Chatur walked out shattered.

The Breakdown Nobody Saw (Except Everyone Did)

He sat under the Great Banyan Tree – the unofficial therapy location for emotional breakdowns.

His thoughts were quiet.

Too quiet.

I don't belong here.

For the first time, he admitted it to himself.

Not angrily. Not dramatically. Just... honestly.

He wasn't cruel. He wasn't ruthless. He wasn't empty.

Which meant he could never win.

The Midnight Resume Resurrection

That night, Chatur opened his laptop.

The security system hooted:

UNAUTHORIZED HOPE ATTEMPT DETECTED. DELETE OPTIMISM? (Y/N)

He clicked *N*.

The system automatically selected *Y*.

After rebooting 14 times, he finally wrote:

Chatur – Business Professional Skilled in Crisis Navigation, Predatory Diplomacy, and Survival Under Absurd Leadership Conditions

He listed achievements:

- Survived hostile negotiations without physical injury
- Reduced screaming trauma by 40%
- Prevented emotional collapse among prey teams
- Convert chaos into outcomes under oxygen deprivation

Skills:

- Advanced disaster response
- High-pressure mediation between carnivores
- Fluent in silence, sarcasm, and screaming
- Resistance to absurdity

Interests:

- Peace
- Sleep
- Breathing without fear

He emailed it across to neighbouring jungles.

Instantly, the screen flashed:

TRAITOROUS ACTIVITY REPORTED TO LEADERSHIP.

Chatur screamed into a pillow.

The pillow screamed back in solidarity.

Cafeteria Confessions

The next morning, he sat silently sipping bitter dew-tea.

A goat sat beside him.

"Rumor says you're leaving," the goat said casually, chewing like existential dread was a flavour.

Chatur froze. "How does everyone already know?"

The goat pointed casually to a fruit basket nearby.

The banana inside crackled like a walkie-talkie and whispered, **"Everything is monitored."**

Chatur flinched so hard he spilled tea onto his own tail.

The raccoon slid into the seat opposite him.

"Smart move, fox. Escape while you still have internal organs functioning. The last guy who tried was promoted."

"To what role?" Chatur asked nervously.

The raccoon leaned in, voice trembling.

"Strategic Vision Alignment."

Chatur swallowed. "What happened to him?"

The raccoon shuddered. "No one knows. The last thing we heard from him was the sound of distant screaming and someone chanting 'alignment' repeatedly."

Across the room, Sunder sneezed violently and a stack of press releases collapsed like a dramatic avalanche.

When the Silver Fox Speaks Truth

Later that day, Chatur found Chalu waiting near the exit.

No audience. No sarcasm. No sharpened words disguised as compliments.

Just honesty.

"Thinking of leaving?" Chalu asked quietly.

Chatur exhaled, weary. "Yes. I think I have to."

Chalu nodded once, slowly.

"I tried once," he said. "Before I became what they needed. Before I learned that this jungle eats hope like snacks at a movie."

Chatur's ears lowered. "Why didn't you leave?"

Chalu laughed – not cruelly, but painfully.

"I didn't know how. By the time I realized what I had become, it was too late. Leaving meant admitting the years were wasted. Staying meant destroying pieces of myself one at a time."

A long silence passed.

"You're lucky, Chatur," Chalu said. "You still have pieces left. Leave before you lose them."

The Decision – Not Dramatic, Just Real

Chatur stepped outside.

The sky looked larger than it ever had. The jungle looked smaller.

He inhaled – not shakily, not desperately – but freely.

I choose myself. I choose peace. I choose the door.

Behind him, the familiar chorus of chaos resumed:

Bolbacchan screaming about ENERGY. Hyenas laughing at nothing and everything. Nishachar threatening to wipe someone from the database. Chakmak declaring an emergency glitter festival.

But none of it reached him anymore.

He just smiled and whispered:

"To greener pastures."

And for the first time since joining Junglee Log –

He felt alive.

******

Chapter 13
The Exit

If corporate life had a natural predator, it wasn't burnout, or markets, or economic downturns.

It was clarity.

And on the morning Chatur decided to leave Junglee Log for good, clarity hit him like a falling coconut.

He woke up before sunrise, and for the first time since joining, his first thought wasn't:

What fresh hell awaits me today?

Instead, it was simple.

I'm done.

The realization arrived not with fireworks, but with quiet relief. His chest felt lighter. His breathing was normal. His tail wasn't twitching in anticipatory trauma. Birds sounded like birds again, not like screaming parrots.

He stretched, drank dew-water, and looked at his reflection in a puddle.

The fox looking back at him wasn't broken.

Just tired.

But behind the exhaustion, there was something new.

Resolve.

"Last month," he told his reflection, "last drama, last circus."

Then he smiled.

And headed for Junglee Log HQ — one last time.

Dropping the Bomb

The HQ clearing hummed with its usual nervous energy. Monkeys were already arguing over whose banana was whose, the hyenas were laughing at something that probably wasn't funny, and the HR squirrel was stress-chewing seed packets at the reception desk.

Chatur walked in like a retired gladiator.

The squirrel squinted at him.

"You look… happy," she said suspiciously.

"I had eight hours of sleep," Chatur replied.

The squirrel dropped her seeds in horror.

"Sleep? On a weekday?"

He smiled kindly and walked past her.

Wordless, he made his way straight to the King's chamber.

Inside, King Chuha Singh sprawled lazily on his polished rock throne, half-listening to Chatu's breathless monologue about "strategic loyalty alignment" while a baby monkey fanned him with a palm leaf.

Chatur bowed.

"Your Majesty," he said.

The king glanced up. "Ah, Chatur. The fox who survives."

Chatu barked proudly, "MY BROTHER! OUR PRIDE! OUR WEAPON!"

Chatur took a breath.

"I'm resigning."

Silence.

A bird flew into a tree.

The baby monkey stopped fanning.

Chatu's tail froze mid-wag.

"Resigning?" the king repeated slowly, like it was a word in a foreign language.

"Yes, Your Majesty," Chatur said. "I've decided to move on. Here is my formal resignation. I'll serve my notice period as required."

He placed a neatly folded leaf-scroll on the stone.

The king stared at it like it was a dead rat.

"But… why?" Chuha Singh asked. "Have we not given you enough challenge? Responsibility? Opportunities to suffer in interesting ways?"

Chatur smiled politely.

"You have," he said. "More than enough. I'm grateful. And done."

The king blinked.

"Is this about money?"

"No."

"Title?"

"No."

"Corner branch office?"

"No."

Chatu jumped in, panicked.

"IS IT ABOUT ME? DID I NOT LOVE YOU LOUDLY ENOUGH??"

Chatur shook his head.

"It's about peace," he said simply.

Something in the king's face shifted.

"Oh," he said quietly. "One of those."

He sighed – not dramatically, but with genuine fatigue.

"Very well," he said. "Submit this to HR. Your notice period is… thirty days."

"Thank you, Your Majesty."

Chatur turned to leave.

"Fox," the king called after him.

"Yes?"

Chuha Singh hesitated.

"Was it really that bad?"

Chatur met his eyes.

He didn't lie.

He didn't rant.

He didn't list every humiliation.

He just said, gently:

"It wasn't good."

And left.

The Parrot Panic

The news reached Bolbacchan approximately six seconds after Chatur stepped out of the king's chamber.

By the time Chatur reached the Sales Den, Bolbacchan was pacing frantically, feathers fluffed, eyes wild.

"NO. NO. NO. THIS IS FAKE NEWS. THIS IS MISCOMMUNICATION. THIS IS A PRANK. THIS IS –"

"True," Chatur interrupted calmly.

"I'm leaving, Bolbacchan. Served my resignation just now."

Bolbacchan froze.

Literally froze.

Like someone had pressed pause.

Then –

"WHAAAAAAAAAT?!?!"

The scream caused three birds to fall out of nearby trees and a distant crocodile to reconsider life choices.

"YOU CAN'T LEAVE! WE ARE IN THE MIDDLE OF A SALES REVOLUTION! THE BEARS LIKE US! THE DEER DON'T CRY AS MUCH! THE HYENAS ONLY BITE TWICE A WEEK NOW! YOU ARE A CORE RESOURCE!!"

Chatur shrugged gently.

"I'll hand everything over properly. You'll manage."

Bolbacchan grabbed his shoulders.

"IS IT THE TARGETS? I WILL REDUCE YOUR TARGETS! I WILL GIVE YOU NEGATIVE TARGETS! I WILL TELL YOU YOU'VE ALREADY ACHIEVED THEM!"

"It's not the targets," Chatur said.

"IS IT ME? I CAN SCREAM LESS! I CAN SCREAM ONLY IN MEETINGS! I CAN TURN MY MOTIVATIONAL PITCH DOWN FROM 100 TO 97!"

Chatur smiled.

"It's not you," he said kindly. "Okay, it's a little you. But it's mostly… everything."

Bolbacchan collapsed to the floor, sobbing.

"This is my fault! I told you to dream big! NOW YOU DREAM OUTSIDE!"

Behind them, one of the warthogs whispered to another, "Mark my words. Next month he'll be screaming into a void with no fox to translate."

The Silver Fox's Reaction

Chalu did not scream.

He did not panic.

He did not beg.

He simply appeared, as he always did, where the story hit its turning point.

Chatur found him standing near the waterhole, watching his own reflection like he was trying to remember who lived inside it.

"I heard," Chalu said quietly, without turning.

"You always do," Chatur replied.

A beat of silence.

"Congratulations," the Silver Fox said.

Chatur frowned. "On resigning?"

"Yes," Chalu said. "On escaping."

He turned, and for the first time since Chatur had joined, the older fox looked… old.

Not in body.

In spirit.

"You did what I never had the courage to do," Chalu said. "You chose the exit while you still recognized yourself."

Chatur swallowed.

"You could still leave," he offered. "You're brilliant. Any jungle—"

"—would see me as a threat," Chalu finished. "Or worse, as a reflection of everything they don't want to admit. No. My roots are here. Rot and all."

A sad smile.

"You don't owe this place anything," he continued. "Serve your notice. Hand things over. Then run. Don't look back. The jungle doesn't remember those who leave. Only those who return."

"Will you be okay?" Chatur asked.

Chalu laughed softly.

"Define 'okay'."

Notice Period: The Great Unravelling

Chatur's notice period started on a Tuesday.

By Wednesday, the jungle was sure of two things:

1. He was definitely leaving.
2. He had stopped giving even the faintest hint of a damn.

A strange freedom descended upon him.

He still came in on time.

He still did his tasks.

But the mask was gone.

No more forced smiles at useless meetings. No more pretending to agree with terrible ideas. No more absorbing emotional damage for the sake of "team spirit."

Instead:

- He declined any meeting without a proper agenda.
- He responded to vague requests with: *"Why?"*
- He replied to passive-aggressive emails with direct questions.
- He stopped saying "Maybe" when he meant "No."
- He stopped offering cover for leadership mistakes.

The most shocking change?

He stopped being afraid of Chatu.

The Chatu Confusion

At first, Chatu reacted to the news like a heartbroken golden retriever.

"BROTHER FOX! SAY THIS IS A JOKE!" he wailed.

"It's not," Chatur said.

Chatu's tail drooped.

"But... but... who will I sit next to in meetings and whisper 'WELL SAID SIR' after everything they say?"

"You could listen to what they're saying," Chatur suggested.

Chatu looked horrified.

"NO! MY ROLE IS TO AGREE!!"

Over the next days, Chatu became weirdly clingy.

He followed Chatur to lunch. He followed him to the wash area. He followed him to sales huddles. He once tried to follow him into the restroom.

"Chatu," Chatur said gently. "I need personal space."

"IS THAT LIKE MEETING SPACE?" Chatu asked.

"In a way," Chatur said. "Only useful."

Something unexpected happened as the days went by.

Chatu's tone changed.

Less shouting. Less blind cheerleading. More... questions.

One afternoon, he whispered:

"Fox... is it really that bad here?"

Chatur didn't answer.

Chatu answered his own question.

"I never thought about it," he admitted quietly. "I was so busy protecting the king... I never asked who was protecting everyone else."

It was the closest thing to self-awareness anyone had ever seen from him.

Bolbacchan on the Edge

The parrot entered denial, then negotiation, then campaign mode.

He called an emergency Sales Town Hall.

"TEAM!" he screamed. "WE ARE LOSING OUR CORE FOX RESOURCE! THIS IS A CRISIS OF TALENT RETENTION, EMOTIONAL ALIGNMENT, AND VOCAL MORALE!!"

The pigeons looked confused.

The deer looked stressed.

The hyenas laughed.

Bolbacchan turned to Chatur.

"WHAT WILL IT TAKE TO MAKE YOU STAY??"

Chatur took the microphone calmly.

"A quiet workplace," he said.

The room laughed.

He did not.

"Fewer useless meetings," he continued.

More laughter.

"A culture that values sanity over chaos," he finished.

Now the laughter died.

Bolbacchan fluffed uncomfortably.

"That sounds... difficult," he admitted.

"Exactly," Chatur replied. "That's why I'm leaving."

The Lion Softens

Chuha Singh, too, began to change.

At first, he tried the usual tactics.

"Stay and I'll give you a grander title."

"What title?" Chatur asked.

"Chief of Something Impressive," the king replied.

"No, thank you."

Then he tried intimidation.

"You realize you may never find a jungle as… dynamic as this?"

"I certainly hope not," Chatur said.

Finally, he tried something unfamiliar.

Honesty.

One evening, as the clearing emptied, Chuha Singh called him aside.

"You were one of the few who actually tried to fix things," the lion said quietly. "Not just decorate them."

"Did it matter?" Chatur asked.

"Yes," the king said. "But not enough."

He sighed.

"This place is older than both of us. Older than its own mistakes. Some jungles don't want to change—they just want to survive until the next crisis."

He looked at Chatur, and for the first time, there was no rank between them.

"Leave," the lion said. "Before this place convinces you that you're the problem."

Exit Mode: Activated

By the last week of his notice period, Chatur had mastered the art of what employees in other jungles called **"reverse working"**.

He still showed up. He still answered questions. He still handed office work.

But his emotional investment had dropped to absolute zero.

Someone asked him to "quickly take ownership" of a new impossible project.

"No," he said.

"Why?"

"I'm leaving in four days."

"Can't you start it?"

"That would be cruel to whoever inherits it."

He sent detailed handover notes to the next poor soul assigned.

******

Chapter 14
Salute to the Rising Sun

Chatur had never known what it felt like to walk into a workplace without immediately wanting to gnaw his own tail off in self-defense. Yet here he was, standing at the gates of **Treehouse Innovations**, staring up at a gorgeous wooden archway adorned with vines, flowers, and a sign that read:

WELCOME, CHATUR – OUR FUTURE LEGEND

He blinked.

He reread it.

He checked behind himself to confirm they weren't expecting another fox.

Nope. Just him.

A drumroll began out of nowhere. A chorus of sparrows burst into synchronized song. A marching band composed of impeccably groomed beavers appeared and began playing triumphant entrance music.

Chatur felt something unfamiliar.

Appreciation.

At Junglee Log, his entrance music was usually Bolbacchan screaming motivational threats at full volume while an owl reset his password for the tenth time.

Here, animals clapped politely and smiled like they genuinely wanted him to exist.

It was unsettling.

In a good way.

Royal Reception

A poised and elegant white crane in a tailored bamboo-fiber blazer stepped forward.

"Chatur, welcome to Treehouse Innovations!" she said, voice smooth as polished mahogany. "I'm **Prakriti**, your onboarding guide."

Onboarding guide? In Junglee Log, onboarding consisted of being thrown into a pit and seeing if you survived.

"Thank you," Chatur said cautiously, waiting for the catch.

Instead, the crane snapped her wings, and six squirrels rolled in a red carpet woven from silk leaves.

"Please," Prakriti gestured, "walk the success path."

He stepped onto the carpet.

Confetti rained down from treetops – soft, quiet, biodegradable confetti. Not glitter designed to blind you emotionally.

A banner unfurled overhead:

OUR NEW STAR HAS ARRIVED ☆

He looked around, bewildered.

A raccoon in uniform offered him a glass of sparkling honey-tonic.

"At Junglee Log," Chatur thought, "I was offered herbal anxiety tea brewed from plants found near accident zones."

Here?

It tasted like hope.

The Grand Introduction Ceremony

In the main clearing, a circular amphi theater had been prepared. Comfortable seating. Soft moss cushions. Ambient forest lighting. No screaming parrots. No involuntary glittering.

Employees stood and applauded as Chatur entered.

A proud-looking elephant wearing reading glasses introduced him:

"Team, it is our honour to welcome **Chatur the Fox**, a brilliant strategist and relationship maestro, known for turning chaos into opportunity."

Applause thundered.

Chatur felt his ears heat.

In Junglee Log, his introduction had been:

"This is Chatur. He will help. Hopefully." – followed by monkey snickering and a falling branch.

Here, employees approached one by one.

"We're so excited to work with you."

"We've heard great things."

"Your Honey Crisis turnaround is legendary."

"Please sit – the head seat is yours."

Head seat.

Last time he sat in a meeting room, his chair had shrunk daily until he was perched on a walnut shell.

Month 1 – The Honeymoon of Productivity

Chatur quickly discovered three astonishing things:

1. **Meetings had agendas.** Real ones.
2. **Emails were respectful and short.** No emotional terrorism.
3. **Workload was realistic.** No "25 deliverables by yesterday" nonsense.

On his first client call, instead of 47 animals screaming conflicting instructions, the team said:

"Feel free to lead the conversation. We trust your expertise."

Chatur choked on his own breath.

Trust?

In Junglee Log, the only thing trusted was that someone would betray someone before the meeting ended.

He presented calmly. The client listened thoughtfully. They asked logical questions.

Afterward, the CEO — a calm, wise-looking tortoise — nodded at him and said,

"Excellent clarity and strategy. You've set a strong foundation."

Chatur nearly fainted.

"Is this real?" he whispered.

Month 1 – Perks That Defied Logic

He received:

- A warm welcome basket
- A meditation hammock

- A personalized mug saying *"Foxes Lead with Intelligence"*
- A wellness stipend for spa mud baths

Spa.

In his old company, the wellness benefit was "permission to cry quietly behind the trees once a week."

His new workstation was ergonomic and comfortable, not a tilted stump.

His laptop login worked every time.

He checked under the desk for hidden sabotage devices.

Nothing.

He asked IT if they needed to inject spyware or emotional damage protocols.

They looked horrified.

"We don't do that here," they said.

Chatur cried.

Softly.

With dignity.

Month 2 – The Golden Fox

By month two, Chatur was a celebrity.

Employees waved warmly when he walked by. Teams competed to collaborate with him. The cafeteria named a smoothie after him: **The Chatur Charge**.

Reviews from leadership glowed like holy sunlight:

"Transformational impact already visible."

"Balances logic and empathy beautifully."

"A leader other leaders look up to."

Back in Junglee Log, his review had said:

"Too emotional. Too honest. Too hardworking. Cultural misfit."

He laughed so hard remembering it he snorted dew-water through his nose.

In a meeting, the Chief Strategy Owl said approvingly,

"You're a fantastic addition. We're lucky to have you."

Lucky.

In Junglee Log the only time he was called lucky was:

"Lucky he hasn't quit yet."

Beauty of Silence

He sat in a meeting room once and listened.

Actual silence.

Not:

- Screaming
- Glitter cannons
- Banana-based microphones transmitting gossip
- Hyenas laughing maniacally

Just thoughtful silence.

He leaned back in his chair, eyes watery.

"This room is soundproof?" he asked.

"Yes," said the squirrel facility manager proudly. "Noise interferes with thinking."

Chatur whispered reverently:

"Blessed be your ancestors."

The Day It Hit Him

One afternoon, after a productive planning session, the CEO called him aside.

"Chatur, how do you feel here so far?"

Chatur considered.

He inhaled. Exhaled. Smiled.

"I feel… safe," he said.

The tortoise nodded.

"That's the first need of leadership. Safety. Growth comes second."

Chatur froze.

Nobody had ever spoken to him like that. Not as a resource. Not as a target number. Not as a tool.

As a creature.

A valid one.

Reflection Night

That evening he sat under a lantern-lit treehouse balcony, sipping honey tonic and looking at the sunset.

He thought of Junglee Log:

Bolbacchan screaming until plants wilted. Nishachar threatening to erase identities. Chakmak throwing glitter at any problem. Chatu saluting anything that moved. The king calling everyone the wrong name. Chalu watching everything burn and calling it strategy.

He laughed.

A long, free, echoing laugh.

"Thank god I left," he whispered.

A passing rabbit asked politely, "Something funny?"

Chatur grinned.

"You wouldn't believe me if I told you."

The Visit of the Hyena

Unexpectedly, on the last day of month two, a visitor appeared.

One of the Hyenas from the Hyena Coalition. Grinning like trouble.

"We heard you escaped," she said.

"I did," Chatur replied proudly.

"How is it on the other side?"

Chatur grinned back.

"Grass is greener. And real. Not spray-painted."

The hyena crackled.

"Good. Keep shining. Some of us need someone on the other side to believe it's possible."

Rising Sun

The next morning, Chatur walked into Treehouse Innovations.

Warm sunrise filtered through golden leaves. The team smiled as he passed.

For the first time in his entire career, he felt not like a survivor — but like a leader.

And he said to himself:

Salute to the rising sun. The dawn after the storm. The chapter where I finally grow.

He looked ahead. He took a deep breath. He stepped forward.

The new day began.

******

Chapter 15
Same Old, Same Old

For six glorious months, Chatur lived inside what felt like a dream. A workplace dream, mind you – not the pleasant flying kind, but the stable, peaceful, breathable kind where no one threw glitter grenades at status calls and parrots didn't scream strategic slogans like a caffeinated war commander.

Treehouse Innovations—the paradise of quiet hallways and reasonable deadlines.

He had learned to sleep. He had learned to exhale. He had learned that applause could be real and not one step away from emotional manipulation.

But as every ancient philosopher (or burnt-out employee) eventually realizes:

There is no such thing as a perfect company.

Because companies are made of animals. And animals are messy.

And slowly, very slowly, things began to shift.

Month 7 – The First Cracks in Heaven's Ceiling

It started when nobody was paying attention.

A tiny change. A minor inconvenience. Barely noticeable.

A meeting invite.

But not just any meeting.

A meeting with the title:

URGENT ALIGNMENT DISCUSSION – NO AGENDA, JUST ENERGY

Chatur stared at the invite like it was a ghost from his past.

"No," he whispered. "Not like this."

He checked the attendees.

Twenty-six animals. No defined speakers. No documents attached.

He checked the duration.

Four hours.

He checked the room name.

'STRESS POD A'

Treehouse Innovations had stress pods now?

He blinked.

"I'll join and observe," he told himself calmly.

But deep inside, something twitched.

The Meeting From Hell (Treehouse Edition)

The meeting began with silence.

Everyone stared at everyone else.

Then someone finally spoke.

"So… why are we here?"

"We're aligning," the beaver manager said confidently.

"On what?"

"That's what we're here to decide."

Heads nodded thoughtfully.

Chatur's eye twitched aggressively.

He asked, carefully:

"Do we have goals? Documents? Problems we're solving?"

"No. We're brainstorming what problems we should brainstorm."

Chatur inhaled slowly.

He began to sweat.

Flashbacks hit like a violent thunderstorm:

Bolbacchan screaming "PASSION!!!" Chakmak throwing glitter into the air. Nishachar resetting his access to **Recycle Bin Only**. King Chuha Singh staring blankly at leaves falling. Chatu drooling loyalty all over his feet.

Chatur's heart rate spiked.

He whispered involuntarily:

"Not again."

The raccoon next to him nodded sympathetically.

"First alignment meeting?"

"Why is this happening?" Chatur breathed.

"It's Q3," the raccoon replied. "Everyone panics in Q3. It's tradition."

Month 7–8 – The Great Confusion Uprising

Like a contagious disease, confusion spread.

Projects duplicated. Priorities changed every 48 hours. Meetings multiplied like termites.

One week they were expanding aggressively. Next week they were cutting budgets. Next week they were expanding again. Then they froze hiring.

The CEO announced:

"We must embrace agile transformation powered by cross-functional resource empowerment!"

Nobody knew what it meant.

The owl wrote it on a whiteboard.

Nobody knew what it meant.

The deer printed it on posters.

Nobody knew what it meant.

The squirrels made T-shirts.

Nobody knew what it meant.

But everyone repeated it passionately because they feared being called out as unaligned.

Chatur attended a strategy session where the only outcome was a unanimous declaration that:

"We must realign alignment."

He cried internally.

Month 8 – Enter the Politics Virus

Internal alliances formed.

Not friendly alliances.

Secretive ones.

The bamboo pandas whispered against the river otters. The squirrels blamed the woodpeckers. The beavers quietly built metaphorical dams of resentment.

Everyone talked about collaboration.

Everyone practiced assassination.

Performance reviews shifted tone. Suddenly, "constructive feedback" meant "we're preparing to sacrifice you for someone else's promotion."

Chatur was pulled into a private call.

"Chatur," said the giraffe director solemnly, "some believe your leadership style is too calm. Too independent. Too quietly competent."

"...Thank you?" Chatur said uncertainly.

"It makes others uncomfortable," she clarified.

Ah.

Competence was a threat. Again.

Month 9 – Clients Discover Stress

External pressure surged.

Three major accounts demanded 72-hour turnaround on unrealistic deliverables.

The hippos wanted comprehensive restructuring models by Tuesday. The wolves needed partnership contracts rewritten overnight. The parrots (different parrots, not Bolbacchan's family) changed requirements 19 times in three days.

Yet every time Chatur asked the leadership for alignment, support, or decisions, the answer was always:

"Let's discuss."

Which ALWAYS meant:

"Let's open another four-hour meeting where nothing happens."

Meanwhile, deadlines burned like unattended campfires.

Stakeholders fought over whose department owned which disaster.

The tortoise CEO started each speech with "Remain calm" – the linguistic equivalent of yelling **EVERYONE PANIC RIGHT NOW!**

Chatur's eyelid began twitching relentlessly.

He drank coffee so strong his soul briefly left his body.

He began using sarcasm as oxygen.

He started narrating his own breakdown in the third person.

"He is trying, universe. He is trying so hard."

Month 9–10 – The Recognition Mirage

He delivered miracles. He saved accounts. He negotiated peace among hostile stakeholders. He pulled 14-hour days.

And received:

- No promotion.
- A generic "Thanks team" email without his name.
- A coffee coupon expiring in three days.

One afternoon he overheard two squirrels whispering:

"Chatur? Is he still here?"

"He works quietly. Sometimes I forget he exists."

He looked at his reflection.

He heard King Chuha Singh's voice echo in his head:

"Was it really that bad?"

He answered, finally:

"It always becomes bad."

Month 10–11 - Emotional Flatline

The cracks became canyons.

He stopped laughing. He stopped hoping. He stopped pretending.

His late evenings became unpaid therapy sessions with his reflection.

"Why do I do this to myself?" he asked the empty room.

His reflection shrugged.

"Because corporate life is an abusive relationship disguised as career progression."

He googled monasteries. He considered yak farming. He fantasized about disappearing into a quiet cave with no WiFi.

Then he remembered something.

A truth so simple it felt illegal:

Every jungle is the same jungle in different packaging.

If you ran far enough, fast enough, long enough—you would still carry yourself.

And if you dragged your panic, expectations, and insecurities with you, the new jungle would rot like the old one.

Maybe the problem wasn't just the jungles. Maybe the problem was the importance he gave them.

The Enlightenment Breakdown

It was during an absurd meeting where 14 animals were passionately arguing about the ideal colour palette for a spreadsheet that something inside Chatur… snapped.

The panda said, "I think mint green is more strongly aligned to brand empathy."

The owl replied, "Research proves teal increases productivity."

The squirrel screamed, "LIME REPRESENTS HOPE!"

The tortoise CEO declared, "We must honour the data-driven emotional spectrum!"

Everyone looked at Chatur.

"What do you think?"

Chatur stood slowly.

Cleared his throat.

And said, through a smile that terrified absolutely everyone:

"I think it's a spreadsheet."

Silence.

Wind.

Somewhere, a leaf fell dramatically.

The room stared.

"That's it," Chatur continued. "It's a spreadsheet. Not a philosophical debate. Nobody's dying. Nobody's saving lives. It's a sheet with rows and columns and colour options.

And it does! not! matter!"

He laughed.

A full, wild, hysterical cackle normally reserved for someone who has seen death and found it boring.

The raccoon clapped slowly.

The rabbit wiped a tear.

The tortoise whispered, impressed and afraid:

"...enlightenment."

Chatur walked out of the spreadsheet-colour war room with the exact expression of someone who had just seen their entire life flash before their eyes – and it was a tragic PowerPoint presentation with no transitions, no animations, and Comic Sans titles.

He didn't slam the door. He didn't scream. He didn't cry.

He simply **laughed**.

A laugh that sounded like a fox who had just achieved spiritual liberation by realizing everything is stupid and nothing matters.

Animals stared as he walked through the hallway giggling like a villain who had finally snapped.

The beavers stopped arguing about KPI ownership. The squirrels froze mid-sentence. The pandas dropped their emotional support bamboo.

Someone whispered, "Is he… having a stroke?"

"No," the raccoon replied, eyes wide with awe. "He's reached enlightenment."

The Enlightenment Moment

He sat under the maple tree outside and stared at the sky.

For months he had been trying to control the chaos – shape it, structure it, improve it.

And now he realized something profound:

Chaos does not want to be controlled. Chaos wants to dance on your corpse wearing glitter lipstick.

He took a deep breath.

Corporate life was not a battle to win. It was a circus to enjoy.

He wrote in his notebook with holy determination:

Rules of Survival

- Care, but casually
- Work hard, but not suicidally
- Smile, especially while saying no
- Meetings are optional; sanity is not
- Don't fix stupid
- Do the job – not the drama

He placed a big box around the last line:

"I will give 100% effort. 0% blood."

He exhaled.

"Same jungle everywhere," he whispered.

"But this time... different fox."

Corporate Zen (Fox Style)

The next day, Chatur arrived at work like a retired warrior who now taught pottery.

Calm. Peaceful. Tail swaying gently like he was floating through lavender fields.

Someone asked urgently:

"Chatur, can you join this emergency call?"

"No," he said gently.

The entire hallway gasped.

"No?"

"Yes," Chatur said serenely. "No."

"Why?"

"Because it's unnecessary."

The raccoon whispered, starstruck:

"He says the forbidden words."

The Spread of the Gospel

He stopped replying to emails marked **URGENT** unless they actually were. He started asking **"Is this real work or emotional theatre?"** before taking tasks. He reduced a four-hour meeting to twelve minutes by asking:

"What exactly are we trying to do?"

Half the room fainted.

The tortoise CEO stared at him like he had invented telepathy.

"Why has no one said that before?" the CEO asked.

"Because everyone is pretending," Chatur said.

One panda broke down crying.

"This fox… he speaks truth."

The Sacred Lesson: Stop Caring Like a Maniac

After two weeks of the New Chatur Era, miracles occurred:

- Deadlines stabilized
- Projects stopped mutating
- Meetings got shorter
- People laughed again
- Nobody threatened to quit during lunch
- No one cried in the restroom

Even the IT owl said,

"I haven't wiped anyone's identity in days. Therapy is working."

One morning the CEO pulled Chatur aside.

"What changed?" he asked.

Chatur grinned.

"Nothing. I just stopped treating work like religion."

The CEO looked emotional.

"My father was a monk," he whispered. "He never said this to me."

The Full Realization

At sunset, Chatur stood on the balcony, looking out over the golden glow of the forest.

He thought of Junglee Log. He thought of Treehouse Innovations. He thought of crisis calls, frantic deadlines, budget battles, performance reviews, and madness disguised as strategy.

And he laughed softly.

It's all the same. Everywhere.

Different animals. Different slogans. Same circus.

The only difference – the performer.

He raised an invisible cup toward the horizon.

"To the same madness," he said.

"And to the new me handling it without losing sanity."

He smiled – not victorious, not resigned, but balanced.

The jungle may never change.

But the fox has.

He walked back inside. Ready.

Not for war. Not for survival.

For peace.

For boundaries.

For himself.

******